kent ira groff

active
spirituality

a guide

for

seekers

and

ministers

an alban institute publication

Grateful acknowledgment is made for use of the following:

Quotation from *Prayer of Jesus: Prayer of the Heart* by Alphonse and Rachel Goettmann. (Mahwah, NJ: Paulist Press, copyright 1991), used by permission.

Quotation from *The Silence of God* by Helmut Thielicke. (Grand Rapids, MI: Wm. B. Eerdmans Publishing Co., copyright 1962), used by permission.

Quotation from *Letters to a Young Poet* by Rainer Maria Rilke. (New York: W.W. Norton, Inc., copyright 1934), used by permission.

Excerpt reprinted from *Luther and the Mystics* by Bengt R. Hoffman, copyright 1976 Augsburg Publishing House. Used by permission of Augsburg Fortress.

Quotation from *Life Together* by Dietrich Bonhoeffer. (New York: Harper & Row Publishers, Inc., copyright 1954), used by permission of HarperCollins Publishers.

Hymns: *When in Our Music God Is Glorified*, words by Fred Pratt Green, copyright 1972; and *God Is One, Unique and Holy*, words by Brian Wren, copyright 1983. (Carol Stream, IL: Hope Publishing Co.), used by permission.

Excerpt from "Little Gidding" in *Four Quartets*, copyright 1943 by T.S. Eliot and renewed 1971 by Esme Valerie Eliot, reprinted by permission of Harcourt Brace & Company. Permission also granted by Faber & Faber, Ltd., London.

Quotation from "Two Tramps in Mud Time," from *The Poetry of Robert Frost* edited by Edward Connery Lathem. Copyright 1936 by Robert Frost. Copyright 1964 by Lesley Frost Ballantine. Copyright 1969 by Henry Holt and Company, Inc. Reprinted by permission of Henry Holt and Company, Inc. Permission for limited distribution in British Commonwealth, Jonathan Cape, Ltd., London

Quotation from "Meditation for a Young Boy Being Confirmed" by Alan Paton. Reprinted by permission of the A.S. Paton Will Trust, Ewing & Swaing, Republic of South Africa.

The Publications Program of The Alban Institute is assisted by a grant from Trinity Church, New York City.

Library of Congress Catalog Card Number 93-73157
ISBN 1-56699-117-X

CONTENTS

INDEX OF PRAYER EXERCISES

Prayer is the chief exercise of faith.
— John Calvin

ACKNOWLEDGMENTS

Acknowledging is strange business. The nighttime sky was important in order for my high school English teacher, the late Laura A. Long, to teach me to ponder and describe its beauty; likewise the Bible was important in order for my late mother, Mary, and Bruce M. Metzger and Robin Scroggs to teach me to look beneath the text and find its meaning.

And I want to acknowledge my strange "call" to this ministry. On the way back from a clergy support group in the early seventies, conversation centered around Transcendental Meditation, which was making it big in Smalltown, USA. I innocently asked, "Why isn't anybody teaching *Christian* meditation?" My Church of the Brethren colleague Sam Flora answered that E. Stanley Jones had combined elements of Christian and Eastern mysticism in the Christian Ashram movement in India. It was a spark that lit a long, slow fire for this minister who did not have a single course on prayer in seminary at Princeton or Chicago.

I owe a debt of gratitude to my dear friend Edwin Sanders, S.J., my first spiritual director; to Tilden Edwards, Gerald May, and Rosemary Dougherty at Shalem Institute in Washington, D.C., and to Diogenes Allen of Princeton Theological Seminary, who introduced this thirsty soul to classical and contemporary ways of living the active-contemplative life. And to the late John Oliver Nelson, founder of Kirkridge Retreat Center, Bangor, Pennsylvania, founding board member of Oasis Ministries, and dear friend and mentor for my retreat ministry.

There are many encouragers: Fredrika, my wife, and my children; they have been bedrock supporters of my crazy praying and writing habits over six years! There is Dorothy Yingling who pointed me to The

---

Alban Institute, and Celia Allison Hahn, my editor, whose guidance and confidence helped me "to speak with my own voice" in these pages.

I could not have written this without my past experiences of ministry: Rochester, New York; Waynesboro and Berwyn, Pennsylvania; Paxton Church, Harrisburg, where my life was tempered and these five goals for spiritual disciplines were born; and Presbyterian Homes, Inc., where Evelyn Shaw, Harold "Skinny" Clough, the late Vincent Ross, and countless pray-ers taught me about suffering love and the spiritual life.

Many have read the manuscript, prayed, and given me valued insight, among them Ray and Phyllis Lindquist, John Seefeldt, Elizabeth Groff, John Norman, Rabbi Carl Choper, and Marcie Larson. I thank Lancaster Theological Seminary, the Center of Continuing Education at Princeton Theological Seminary, Chautauqua Institution, and scores of churches and retreat settings where clergy and lay folks have been my teachers, enriching what you will experience as you "retreat" with this book.

—Kent Ira Groff

INTRODUCTION

One Sunday night, a middle-aged layperson who had spent most of his adult life working professionally for an agency of his church wrote his pastor:

> *You saw me in church today as I usually am when I'm in town. I sang the hymns and prayed the responses, but I was just mouthing the words. I listened to the Scriptures and sermon, but nothing seemed to connect. It's not the fault with your sermons, but the meaning just isn't there anymore. When I try to pray on my own, it feels dry and empty . . . .*
>
> *Sincerely,*

After a time with no response, he invited the pastor to lunch. When still no mention was made of his letter, he approached the subject: "I'm puzzled. I wrote and bared my soul to you, but you haven't responded."

"I know," the pastor confessed. "I sing the hymns and read the Scriptures and preach the sermons and try to pray, and it seems dry. And I'm a minister. I feel the same way, and I didn't know what to say."

After telling this at a retreat, I asked, "What do you think this story has to say about spirituality or ministry or friendship?"

One person responded, "What a pity. The minister didn't share because he was afraid to admit he felt the same way. But if he could have, maybe they could have helped each other."

One Beggar Showing Another Beggar

We are all continually seeking *and* ministering. The story illustrates how often religious professionals and church members stand on common ground before the cross if they only knew it. Christian spirituality is "one beggar showing another beggar where to find bread," to recast an ancient proverb. An experience of dryness can become an invitation to deepen a spiritual friendship. What if these two could have covenanted to meet together regularly for a while—and to pray for each other between meetings, to read a book and discuss it, or to go on a retreat together?

A spiritual emergency can become the occasion for spiritual emergence! But without vulnerability we stand at a distance when there could be spiritual intimacy. The vital nerve of faith is pinched, almost severed, but we develop an emotional Novocain to avoid our spiritual pain. Meanwhile we just keep on producing things faster and saying them louder—all the while knowing more is not always better.

A Spiritual Emergency

The opening story is not an isolated case. *There is a spiritual emergency in the church today.* "Whenever there is a crisis in the church, it is always here: a crisis in contemplation," wrote Carlo Carretto.[1] Contemplation looks in two directions: You can contemplate the beauty of a rosebud or the pain of an accident. Failure to contemplate the hurt of others manifests itself in acts that never connect with the real needs of the people we serve; failure to contemplate the deep Mystery of God's love manifests itself in irrelevant theology and boring worship.

Many of my clergy contemporaries—and now consequently many people in our pews—have never explored the roots of their own spirituality. During the "secular sixties" I did not have even one course on prayer during my three years in seminary or two years in a doctoral program in religion. And only recently did I discover that I had no underlinings or highlights in the longest single chapter of John Calvin's *Institutes of the*

Christian Religion: "Prayer, Which Is the Chief Exercise of Faith, and by Which We Daily Receive God's Benefits." The professor admits he never assigned it—an omission he says he later corrected.

Yet even with a renewed interest in spirituality, fear is still our enemy. Some are afraid that anything "spiritual" will smack of New Age crystals or cults; others fear that yesterday's musty piety might dull the cutting edge of social action. Clergy worry lest far-out books get into the hands of "our" members! But heresy—distorted belief—is always *an exaggeration of some neglected portion of the truth.*

So whenever the churches neglect a healthy, balanced mysticism, people frantically grasp for it elsewhere in unhealthy, imbalanced proportions: Witness the presence of so many cults. Albert Schweitzer—physician, theologian, musician, and mystic—represented "mystical devotion in its best sense, within the total stream of human events," as Georgia Harkness put it in *Mysticism: Its Meaning and Message.* Today one surely thinks of Mother Teresa in Calcutta.

Active Spirituality: For Seeking *and* Ministering

But a balanced spirituality is not just for a few extraordinary people. We all seek *and* minister. Facing an insecure future after caring for a learning-disabled son for three decades, a mother said, "It's not that I don't believe or pray anymore, but my faith is numb." And as the earlier story illustrates, pastors are not immune to such spiritual burnout. It is both an occupational hazard and blessing that we must preach to others even in our own "dark night of the soul." There is a gap between our believing in Christ (part 1 of this book) and our following Christ (part 2).

So why another book on spirituality? How is this one different from other good ones?[2] An overwhelming majority of Americans *believe* in a personal God according to pollster George Gallup, and a majority of these say they *believe* in Jesus Christ. These are the people joining and serving our churches and going to seminary, but they are struggling with, What does it mean to say, *I believe?* and, What do you do after you say, *I believe*, to keep the flame of faith alive?

Using seven simple themes, this book provides a unique perspective on the complexities of *both* our re-turning home *and* our training for the journey. Most books addressing themes of Christian spirituality presume the reader is a Christian already, yet in Kierkegaard's words, one is *becoming a Christian* all one's life! Or some books are so blandly generic that they lose the Christian focus; others are so narrowly "Christian" that they miss our own "Eastern" heritage. Some are mainly readings *about* spirituality for the "left brain"; others are mainly prayer exercises for the "right brain." Some emphasize prayer unhooked from service and learning. Here are unique ingredients of *Active Spirituality:*

☐ It is *Christian.* The Christ-life is both the Source and the Pattern for the believer and the believing community, following the classical theme of *the imitation of Christ.*

☐ It is *ecumenical*, emphasizing Orthodox and Reformation tradition of growing in the community of faith. Yet it integrates evangelical, Wesleyan, Quaker, African-American, Catholic—especially Ignatian spirituality—and Eastern mystical themes related to the Bible, just as Paul integrated "secular" poets in his teaching (Acts 17:22-28).

☐ It is *paradoxical*, keeping the creative tension between solitude and community, personal faith and service in the world, the intellectual and mystical, the sensual and spiritual. As I thumb through the Bible, always open beside a small icon of Christ next to my computer, I look around and see in my mind analogies in art, sports, music, poetry, literature—in someone's face or in the silence.

☐ It is *experiential.* To read about prayer without praying would be a "theological oxymoron"—like taking chemistry without the laboratory experiments! The prayer exercises are not an appendage: They are integral for the reader, alone or with friends, to know God rather than merely know theology. The way to learn from the One who said "I am the journey" (John 14:6) is by going on the journey.[3]

☐ To limit our task would be easier. It seems an impossible challenge to relate spirituality to *every area of one's life* in the church and in the world. Yet that *is* our vocation: *Turn to God in all things, in all things to see God.*

So now, with the aid of Scripture, spiritual writings, spiritual friends, and your own experience, we will explore the mystery of how the spark of faith ignites (part 1) and disciplines that keep the flame burning (part 2). To use another metaphor, we will explore, and I hope deepen, the roots of faith so we can cultivate the fruits of love.

PRAYER EXERCISE 1: What Does It Mean to Believe?

Reflect prayerfully on your answers to these two basic questions of our inquiry: What does it mean *to you* to say, *I believe?* What are some specific ways that help *you* to "practice the presence" after you say, *I believe?*

Try writing your reflections in your journal. (If you don't have one, go to the nearest newsstand and invest in an empty "write-your-own book.") Then find a friend, family member, or group and share your reflections.

Textual Note

Throughout the book, ☐—open squares—rather than numerals are used to convey a series of points in sequence, since so often (1) is not more important than (3). For the same reason, ●—bullets—are used as sub-sets that might be (a), (b), (c), or for briefer series' of points. Bullets are used in prayer exercises to convey sequential movements.

Part I
Re-Turning Home

Roots of Faith: What Does It Mean to Believe?

Theme 1
Homesickness

CHAPTER I

Stirrings

The world breaks everyone and afterward many are strong at the broken places.

—Ernest Hemingway, *A Farewell to Arms*

Everyone is homesick. Whether you have experienced a "leap of faith" —or even a slow walk into faith—you must have felt some kind of stirring just to open these pages. Or you may not think you are "religious" at all and find yourself surprised to be reading this, though you may in fact be very spiritual. Others may have grown up in the church and left—or left and returned. Or you may see yourself as a committed Christian, lay or clergy. Life is beckoning everyone.

Two Kinds of Strugglers

There are two ways of coming to believe. Some have a life-altering conversion and can point to the day and the hour; they are "Paul" Christians (Acts 9, 22, 26). But "Timothy" Christians have an equally genuine faith nurtured from childhood, like the young adult to whom Paul wrote—or someone echoing Paul: "I am reminded of your sincere faith, a faith that lived first in your grandmother Lois, and your mother Eunice, and now, I am sure, lives in you" (2 Timothy 1:5; see also 3:15).

All of us have one thing in common, dramatically converted or gradually converted: We are all struggling–seeking *and* ministering. "For this I toil and struggle with all the energy that [Christ] powerfully inspires within me" (Colossians 1:29). So if God's love in Christ is a gift, then even *the struggle,* even *the desire* to keep the flame of faith alive is a gift.

Grieving Our Way toward Believing

People talk about believing all the time. What do they mean? *Belief* is the most common word for *faith* or *trust* in Hebrew and Greek. Though belief may seem less personal, that is precisely where a lot of people start—the ninety-some percent who answer a Gallup poll as having at least a generic "belief in God."[1] Folks will say, "I believe" (*credo* in Latin) to refer to God on Sunday, and again on Monday to express their opinions about the weather or the next election.

But the origin of be-*lieve* is intensely personal, from the Old English *leof*, meaning "dear, cherished, loved, or longed for." Add the prefix *be*—meaning "to cause to be"—and what we cherish causes our be-ing, makes us who we are. We become what we long for.

To pray is to yearn. Everyone, in that sense, is "praying"; it is simply the word we use to express that primal longing for what we cherish deeply. "Believing" occurs *when we consciously affirm that deep longing*. It may or may not be named as "Christian" believing, for there are primal spiritual stirrings common to all people. The New Testament shows us that such generic yet genuine yearnings of God-honoring people can begin with awareness of the Divine and lead to a personal experience of believing in Jesus Christ.[2]

Much of our yearning is for cherished experiences we feel we have lost. We begin the process of grieving in childhood. Being weaned from a mother's breast and learning to walk involve loss of an infant's intense intimacy and security; a new sibling means some loss in status; a new school or a move brings loss of friendships. Most obvious are the painful separations through divorce or death. Abused children grieve the loss of a fantasy of being a family like the Brady bunch or the Partridge family.

Our grieving creates a longing until our believing begets our belonging. Out of these painful longings we develop new beliefs, new cherished experiences. Here is the deep mystery: Death and the many little deaths of our lives become the doorway to growth and new life. This is what my Jesuit friends call the paschal mystery, from *Pascha*, the Hebrew Passover, where violent political oppression in Egypt becomes the birthpangs of liberation. The paschal mystery is seen most clearly in the cross and resurrection of Jesus: Violent suffering is transformed into loving energy. It is the message of the Joseph story in Genesis: "You meant it for evil, but God meant it for good, so that many people might be kept alive" (Genesis 50:20 RSV).

But if we do not fill the vacuum of our losses with positive beliefs, it becomes filled with misbeliefs, what psychologists call cognitive distortions. We clutch these "attachments" to fill the void, until one by one they disillusion us. But if we will stop to listen to our grieving, our temporary desires point us to our deepest Desire.

Ancient Words: Fresh Vocabulary

The ancient themes of "being lost on a journey" and "coming home" are primary images for "sin" and "salvation" throughout the Bible. Yet these are also fresh metaphors for our own time of radical mobility—major themes in the stories of John Cheever, Flannery O'Connor, Ernest Hemingway, and Walker Percy. Anne Tyler combines the two images in the title of her novel *Dinner at the Homesick Restaurant.*

The term *home* has a long history. Home was the center of the world, the place where the vertical path up to the sky and down to the underworld crossed with the horizontal line representing the traffic of the earth. After leaving home, every sojourner knew it was impossible to return to the exact place where the two lifelines crossed. Describing our century, John Berger writes, "The one hope of creating a center is to make it the whole earth. Only worldwide solidarity can transcend modern homelessness."[3]

I recently returned to the farmhouse in Chester County, Pennsylvania, that I called home from age five until I was married. The house had been restored, but the barn had been razed and two housing developments covered the rolling meadows and fields! I *felt* the truth of the words of Thomas Wolfe: *You Can't Go Home Again.*

But even if we could reconstruct the *atmosphere* of early "home," it is never the ideal we fantasized. In real life, "coming home" is a negative image for many. Yet strangely, the more terrible and traumatic one's actual experience of home, the greater that person's fantasy of what home *ought* to be, therefore the greater the spiritual homesickness.

That is why our homesickness is so universal and unsolvable, reflected in the words of the German poet Novalis: "Philosophy is really homesickness, it is the urge to be at home everywhere." The fairy tale genre of literature reflects our hunger to come home to the beautiful self somewhere at the root of *each of us* yet mysteriously connected to *all of us*. Bruno Bettelheim's observation in *The Uses of Enchantment* strikes a universal chord: that the fairy tale will continue to speak in every age of life because it expresses the monsters and fantasies in all of us.

PRAYER EXERCISE 2: Spiritual Self-Esteem

Before we further explore the theme of pilgrimage, I invite you to meditate on a passage from Isaiah to renew your sense of being created uniquely in the image of God (Genesis 1:26) and to touch that yearning to be restored to that unique self.

This is "prayer in reverse," so to speak—if you usually think of prayer as speaking to God. Engage in this "listening prayer" as if God is speaking directly to you. Jacob/Israel originally was the name of an individual, but it also became the name of the people of God. So wherever you read "Jacob" or "Israel," hear your first name, then perhaps your full name.

Pray this passage:

> **Thus says the Lord,**
>   **... who created you, O [Jacob] ____,**
>   **... who formed you, O [Israel] _____:**
> **Do not fear, for I have redeemed you;**
>   **I have called you by name ____ you are mine.**
> **When you pass through the waters, I will be with you;**
>   **and through the rivers, they shall not overwhelm you;**
> **when you walk through the fire you shall not be burned,**
>   **and the flame shall not consume you.**
> **For I am the Lord your God,**
>   **the Holy One of Israel, your Savior . . . .**
> **You are precious in my sight,**
>   **and honored, and I love you . . . .**

Can a woman forget her nursing child,
  or show no compassion for the child of her womb?
Even these may forget,
  yet I will not forget you.
See, I have inscribed [your name ___] on the palms of my hands
  (Isaiah 43:1-4; 49:15-16).

Does any particular phrase beckon you, implanting itself in your mind and heart? If so, stay with that phrase; carry it with you, recalling it, repeating it in rhythm to your breathing. Pray these verses each week until you memorize them. Come back to this "prayer" whenever you find your self-esteem being chipped away. *You are precious in my sight and honored, and I love you.* Tasting how deeply I am loved causes me to re-turn homeward.

Biblical Images: Journey and Home

All we have to do is open the Bible, and we are greeted by a Gospel proclamation in the title of the first book of the Torah, Genesis—"beginnings": We can *begin the journey again!* In texts familiar to the most secular Americans, the twin images of *journey* and *home* leap out from the pages of Scriptures from Genesis to Revelation.

☐ The Garden of Eden presents a deep image of home that beckons us, in Milton's phrase, to a *Paradise Lost.* We now feel rootless and restless, yet it was necessary to leave home. The aging Abraham and Sarah were called to risk a *journey* away from their security to a *homeland* that God would give them. The young Joseph grew up in a dysfunctional family and was sold into slavery by his siblings. But providentially his "bad trip" was used for good: Later during a famine, Joseph provided food for alien Egyptians and his own alienated kin in Egypt; in a painful reconciliation, the family came "home" even in a strange land.

☐ Over centuries they became enslaved in Egypt. Moses led the Exodus *journey* out of oppression, through forty years of wilderness sojourning until they entered the Promised Land: a new home. In the regal period, the people built and then rebuilt a "house for the Lord," while the people's *creed* was "A wandering Aramean was my ancestor,

[who] went down to Egypt and sojourned there, few in number . . . " and their *ethic* was "Love the sojourner therefore; for you were sojourners in the land of Egypt" (Deuteronomy 26:5; 10:19 RSV).

☐ Later, the people were forced to leave home and live in exile in Babylon as sojourners again: "How could we sing the Lord's song / in a foreign land?" (Psalm 137:4). Then they journeyed home again to re-build and replant: "In *returning and rest* you shall be saved; / In *quiet-ness and in trust* shall be your strength" (Isaiah 30:15, italics added). But as the parallel phrase indicates, their "re-turning" was to be a spiri-tual homecoming, not merely a geographical one.

☐ Psalm 23 contains these twin themes, beginning with a *journey*: following the gentle Shepherd's paths in green pastures, beside still waters, then through the valley of deep darkness. It ends with a table spread, a cup overflowing, at *home* with God forever.

☐ All four Gospels are written like dramas: In a journey through conflict, pain, and joy, the reader is drawn into the plot—a literary for-mat unique in the ancient world, much like a contemporary historical novel. Particularly Luke the Physician emphasized hospitality while on the journey. Mary and Joseph journeyed under political oppression to *Bethlehem*—in Hebrew meaning *house of bread*—and the Messiah was born in a "feeding trough" in a borrowed *guest house* (Luke 2). In the Matthew account the holy family was forced to journey down to Egypt as political refugees from King Herod (Matthew 2). In all four gospels Jesus' ministry is a series of journeys leading to *the final journey* to the cross. At the very heart of Luke's Gospel are two great parables: the Good Samaritan who carries to a *guest house* a man wounded on a *jour-ney* (Luke 10), and the Prodigal Son who *journeys* to a far country, comes to himself, and then returns *home* to the waiting father (Luke 15). Luke ends his Gospel with two disciples journeying to the *village* (Greek *kome*) of Emmaus. Their hospitality—extended to a "stranger" in a guest house while "on the way"—becomes a homecoming with the risen Messiah!

☐ Luke tells us in his first book about "all that Jesus began to do and teach" (Acts 1:1 RSV); in his second—the Acts of the Apostles—he writes about all that the risen Christ continues "to do and teach" through the journeys of his messengers, *the followers of the Way*. The Christian religion itself is even referred to as *the Way—the Journey* , the meaning of the Hebrew *halacha* (Acts 9:2; 19:23; 22:4). In John's Gospel, Jesus uses the term to identify himself: "I am the *journey*, and the truth, and the life" (14:6, adapted). The early Christians met in *house churches* (Acts 2:2; 16:40; Romans 16:5) as well as in the temple.

☐ The final book of the Bible, next to the last chapter, proclaims: *God's home is with mortals!* (Revelation 21:3).

These images resonate with our experience of life's paradoxical rhythm of adventure and security. We are all in some way wounded on our journey and yearn to return to a spiritual respite (part 1 of this book). But the metaphors also provide a model for keeping us open to fresh experiences of grace along the journey, creatively balancing the disciplines of community and solitude, learning and service (part 2). To mix the alternate metaphors, we return home to our spiritual roots to cultivate the fruits of love on our active journey.

Blessing through Brokenness: The Paschal Mystery

"The world breaks everyone and afterward many are strong at the broken places." Hemingway's words echo the paschal rhythm of brokenness and blessing in our lives. We get wounded like the man traveling from Jerusalem to Jericho who did a dumb thing—setting out alone and on a known dangerous road (Luke 10:29-37).[4] Each of us has dare-devilishly taken a lonely road if we have ever lived. But the evil robbers were *not* of the sojourner's doing. Similarly, we are most often wounded by some combination of foolish things of our own doing and external circumstances beyond our control.

But we are saved by surprise: Compassion does not always come from the expected sources—priest, Levite, institutional religion. Actually, some of our wounds have come from rejections when the institutional church has "passed us by," ignoring our need and walking past on the other side of the road. It is sad yet encouraging to know that gifted spiritual guides—Francis of Assisi, Meister Eckhart, Julian of Norwich; Blaise Pascal, Sören Kierkegaard, and Simone Weil[5]—were "bypassed" by the institutional church of their time. Like resident aliens, many people of prayer have engaged in a lover's quarrel with the church.

Often divine compassion comes through a "smarting Samaritan" wounded healer.

This is truly the paschal *mystery*: How is it that blessing comes through brokenness? Why is it only that *some* grow strong? How is it that "many are called, but few are chosen" (Matthew 22:14)? Some become still weaker before they grow strong; some become bitter. Maybe it has to do with our receptivity to grace through the cross-coming to us by surprise through some "Samaritan" person or experience. It also has to do with deliberately *taking up one's own cross* and following Christ.

To "take up" means to *embrace one's brokenness* rather than running from it, but that is not the same as passive resignation. For now, we need to explore ways the world breaks us—if we are to face our homesickness squarely—to embrace that *deep desire* to return to our true Home. Only then can we develop disciplines to become strong at the broken places.

PRAYER EXERCISE 3: Meditating with Christ on the Cross

Become aware of some brokenness in your own life, past or present, or of some brokenness in another's life that is causing you pain. Now visualize Christ on the cross, sharing that brokenness with you.

Protestants emphasize Christ's resurrection and often do not have or appreciate the use of a crucifix. Yet Martin Luther continued to use a crucifix as a meaningful aid to prayer. And Paul wrote, "We proclaim Christ crucified" (1 Corinthians 1:23).

You don't need a crucifix to create your own inner visualization of Christ sharing your pain on the cross. For example, if you are experiencing a painful relationship—with a child, partner, friend, or co-worker—*visualize Jesus on the cross sharing the pain that you feel over that relationship*. Continue to picture Christ still wounded yet risen, saying to you as a "doubting Thomas": *See my hands and feet* (John 20:25-27; see also Luke 24:30).

For a more extended experience: Try to spend five minutes with this exercise daily or several days a week for about a month.

CHAPTER II

Our Incurable Godsickness

*I thought I would feel guilty. But I didn't feel guilty at all. What I felt
was lonely.*
                    —Peter, in John Cheever's "A Boy in Rome"

We can become so adept at concealing our emptiness. A respected
professional revealed a nasty habit of biting the nails on his left hand.
He would curl the fingers in so no one noticed, but many times they
remained raw and sore. While others saw him as successful and "well-
healed," as he discussed his life he began to relate that he felt a gnawing
spiritual soreness.

Dis-illusionment: Opening to the Real

Homesickness is a condition where the self I know and live with feels
estranged from—even unaware of—my ideal self. The inner emptiness
is what the Bible means by "sin"—a low-grade spiritual *dis-ease*. This
estrangement is threefold: from self, others, and God. Its external symptoms are labeled "sins"—such as killing, rape, cheating, deceit, prejudice.
But before sin is an act, it is a state of being.[1]

The inner awareness of brokenness starts much earlier than one's
thirties, as commonly accepted—in adolescence for many: Witness the
teen suicide rate. "It is an illusion that youth are happy, an illusion of
those who have lost it," wrote Somerset Maugham.[2] And *the actual
experience* of destructiveness begins in early childhood, unspoken or
unawares.

Our "incurable God-sickness" may temporarily seem to be "cured" by
drugs or alcohol, career achievement, a larger home, a new relationship, a

---

new marriage, the coming of a child, a new leisure activity, or some *cause celebre,* even one for the good of the social order! But sooner or later we discover that *even the good things* may be addictions—and may disappoint us.[3]

Attachment to the "dead experiences" of our past *wounds or successes* becomes the way of spiritual death, and detachment becomes the seedbed for genuine life.

> A leaf that has served its purpose
> as a thing of beauty
> can only become
> nurturing
> humus
> when it
> leaves:
> detaching
> as it grieves,
> it fails and falls
> to the Ground of its being
> to nurture another thing of beauty.

To be dis-illusioned is to be freed from illusions and open to the Real. To act as if my "world" is the center of the universe is an illusion: Since Copernicus we have understood this scientifically, but it is painful to learn it spiritually. We experience this disillusioning in three areas: *in relationships, in vocational goals,* and through *death-confronting experiences.* A relationship with another—or with God—disappoints you; technology makes your job obsolete; a loved one is killed in a car crash.

Eventually, at least at death if not in life, we will finally let go of all our attachments. Jesus' message is, *Do not wait for the crisis.* We become truly blessed if we learn the art of detachment—letting go of illusion–while we are still living. The truly fortunate are "the poor in spirit" who hunger and thirst for *what is truly important* (Matthew 5:1-11).

Loneliness: Birthpangs of Homecoming

In our day loneliness rather than guilt is often the first sign of spiritual reawakening. In John Cheever's story "A Boy in Rome," Peter decides to play hooky from school and gets a job as a guide for a tour company named Roncari. Peter comes home at nights, pretending to his mother that he is going out to school each morning. Then he reveals what was happening inside him: "I thought I would feel guilty, but I didn't feel guilty at all. What I felt was lonely."[4]

But instead of facing our loneliness as a spiritual symptom, we substitute novelty in the form of job, things, degrees, or even religion to fill the vacuum. Our way to satisfaction is always to add on: More is better. To believe in the wounded Messiah is an invitation to face the loneliness squarely instead of masking it, to embrace it as our cross and surrender it: "[Abba], into your hands I commend my Spirit" (Luke 23:46). Surrendered loneliness is like the beauty of the Grand Canyon: A wound on the environment of our lives can become an inexhaustible treasure of beauty and self-understanding.[5] This is a meaning of the *Beatitudes*—the *beautiful thing* within each of us is often born out of poverty of spirit.

Homesickness: Two Expressions

Growing up, I got conflicting messages about God. On the one hand, we were taught to "lead a good Christian life"—basic faith and morality, all decently and in order, Presbyterian style. We learned our prayers and scriptures, including John 3:16 and the Golden Rule. On the other hand, we learned that none of these good things could bring us closer to God or "save us." God's love was a gift and the best prayer was that of the tax collector in the temple: "God, be merciful to me, a sinner!" (Luke 18:13). Although this conflict would help me grow, it reached a crisis in my teen years. Through parachurch groups such as Youth for Christ and Inter-Varsity Christian Fellowship, I quickly realized that the people with the most dramatic "testimonies" had led the wildest lives! If I would just accept Christ, by saying a sinner's prayer or accepting four spiritual laws or going to "the altar," then I too could give an exuberant testimony. But unless I got into some really big trouble, I still would not have a dramatic story to tell. I began to feel guilty for believing I was a Christian!

A century-and-a-half ago Horace Bushnell wrote in *Christian Nurture* about this rift between suddenly converted "Paul" Christians and gradually converted "Timothy" Christians. This New England "Puritan" pronounced freedom for kids like myself who grew up in church never knowing a time when we were not Christians. Simultaneously, in the seminary of the German Reformed Church, then at Mercersburg, Pennsylvania, William Nevin and Philip Schaff emphasized *growth in grace through the life and liturgy of the believing community.* "The Mercersburg Theology" is still part of the "curriculum" at Mercersburg's continuing institution, Lancaster Theological Seminary, where I teach. Both the Puritan and German Reformed streams, now the United Church of Christ, offer a rich tradition for "Timothy Christians" who grew up in "sincere faith" at a grandparent's knee (2 Timothy 1:5).[6]

As an adult I would discover the seventeenth-century French scientist and mystic Blaise Pascal, who named what I felt in those pressured adolescent years: "The Way of God, who disposes all things with gentleness, is to instil religion into our minds with reasoned arguments and into our hearts with grace, but attempting to instil it into hearts and minds with force and threats is to instil not religion but terror." Eventually though painfully, at the time without benefit of the above theological perspectives, I concluded that like Timothy I had been a Christian from childhood.[7]

Within Baptist and Anabaptist communities there has been an unwritten tradition of a youthful "sowing your wild oats" as a prelude to radical conversion. But it often promoted a double-standard: "Wild oats" were more acceptable for men than women. In some ways the model of youthful extravagance and later conversion is similar to the twin Hindu teachings: the path of desire and path of renunciation, illustrated by Hermann Hesse's *Siddartha.*[8]

What I did not understand in my youth, not till many years after seminary, was that my worldly friends who had undergone dramatic conversion experiences and I with my sincere growing faith were experiencing *two classical spiritual paths.*

One is the *kataphatic path*, a movement *toward* the world; the other is the *apophatic path*, a movement *away* from the world. They are sometimes called the *via positiva* and the *via negativa*, the affirmative way and the negative way. The first is the way of self-fulfillment and attraction to images and pleasures.[9] It is a whole-hearted embracing of the world, living life *sensuously*, and it becomes the way of the cross that breaks some. The second is the way of self-denial and negation. It is a turning away from the world's pleasures, living life *seriously*, yet it too becomes the way of the cross that breaks some; religious perfectionism can be the root of much destructive pain. These two ways can shed light on our being without Christ as well as our being in Christ. They illumine two ways of our being lost and also two ways to grow in grace, illustrated by the following paradoxical ideas from Christian tradition:

☐ *Christianity is the most materialistic of the world religions* (a theme of William Temple, the late archbishop of Canterbury). Here is the message of Christmas, the Incarnation, the Word made flesh, and of Easter, the Word resurrected in flesh again; it is the Holy present in the sensuous images of nature, the wonders of science and technology, the beauty of music and art, the miracle of the human body and brain. "The Child of Humanity came both eating and drinking" (Matthew 11:19).[10] It is the affirmative path.

☐ Yet the message of the negative path is also valid. In the words of Meister Eckhart: *God is not found in the soul by adding anything but by a process of subtraction.* Here is Lent, Jesus at prayer in the wilderness fasting from the bread of worldly pleasure, power, and prestige; it is Good Friday where this strange Messiah bids us join in the path of denial: "If any want to become my followers, let them deny themselves and take up their cross and follow me" (Mark 8:34).

Sometimes the two paths take on a rhythm in our lives:

For everything there is a season,
and a time for every matter under heaven:
a time to be born, and a time to die;
a time to plant, and a time to pluck up what is planted;
a time to kill, and a time to heal;
a time to break down, and a time to build up;

a time to weep, and a time to laugh;
a time to mourn, and a time to dance;
a time to throw away stones, and a time to gather stones together;
a time to embrace, and a time to refrain from embracing;
a time to seek, and a time to lose;
a time to keep, and a time to throw away;
a time to tear, and a time to sew;
a time to keep silence, and a time to speak;
a time to love, and a time to hate;
a time for war, and a time for peace (Ecclesiastes 3:1-8).

Surely certain personality types are more prone to one path than the other. There may be longer and shorter chapters of each at certain points in our lives. And surely too, we can be equally lost during our times of embracing the world's success as in times of losing it.

Prodigals and Perfectionists: Two Ways of Being Lost

At the center of each of these seemingly opposite paths is a common experience of lostness: an inner homesickness *for some primal childlike innocence or for some youthful idealism.* It is a "homing instinct" for peace or the "tiger instinct" for potency—or both at once.

There is solid biblical tradition for these two ways of responding to our lostness highlighted in the parable of the Prodigal and the Perfectionist (Luke 15:11-32). The Prodigal's is the way of falling in love with the world's pleasures. "Prodigal" is related to "prodigy," and often it is the highly gifted person who seems to embrace the world wildly and waste those gifts: "He squandered his property in [reckless] living" (v. 13). Then there is the dutiful older sibling whose way is that of self-denial. This is the Perfectionist who stays secure at home but fails to claim his gifts, his father saying, "You are always with me, and all that is mine is yours" (v. 31).

Both siblings distance themselves from the genuine and generous goodness of the father. The Perfectionist though physically close to the parent at home is emotionally and spiritually far away. Picture yourself in a situation where you experienced a strained relationship: Emotional distance can actually be more painful than geographical distance. Sin is not being *far* from God; it is turning our gaze in the wrong direction.[11]

The Wayward Child sins by his own fault, the Dutiful Child by default. One sins *willfully*, demanding his share of the property. The other sins *by lack of will*, failing to claim his gifts: " . . . all that is mine is yours."

But our homecoming begins with re-turning our gaze in the right direction. The moment the Prodigal "came to himself" (v. 17), in his mind he was already home even while still in the far country. Repentance (Greek *metanoia*) means "re-turning the mind, making an about face in one's heart." Salvation is an ongoing process of repentance: We *have been* saved; we *are* saved; and we *will be* saved.[12] Salvation is becoming whole and holy—continually re-turning the mind and heart in the right direction.

Salvation starts with contemplation: *When he came to himself* the Prodigal had begun to turn his gaze in the right direction. But when the Perfectionist for once left his work (his addiction!) and *actually came to the house—*even in envy and anger refusing to go in—*he too had begun to turn his gaze in the right direction*; by contemplating his anger at least there was movement. Even our imperfect re-turning movements expose us to God's initiative: "His father came out and began to plead with him" (v. 28). So if our gaze is turned toward the face of God, even in anger, the word of grace can draw us the rest of the way home: "You are always with me" (v. 31).

The Prodigal contemplates, "How many of my father's hired hands have bread enough and to spare?" (v. 17). The Perfectionist contemplates the gaiety of his brother's party, then finally explodes: "For all these years I have been working like a slave for you. . . . But when this son of yours . . . " (v. 29).

In both cases sensual self-interest triggers this "revelation": That no-good is better off than I am! For the Prodigal who had embraced the world, the spiritual re-turn begins by contemplating *how sad* he was: Slaves were better off. Broken by the outward path of worldly pleasure, his healing begins by withdrawal, a movement inward.

But for the Perfectionist who had never embraced the world, the spiritual re-turn began by contemplating *how mad* he was: The father's party for his brother was unfair. Broken by too much self-sacrificing, his healing begins with a movement outward, confronting head-on his own secret yearning for the world's pleasures.

To both the Wayward Child and the Dutiful Child the good news comes through an occasion of pain. *It is the same message, but for differing needs.* To the wounded Prodigal, the message comes: "You have wasted your gifts! Pigs and hired servants have made you aware of your emptiness." *You are forgiven! Come home to love!*

To the wounded Perfectionist, the message is "Your anger has made you aware of your emptiness. You are always with me, and all that is mine is yours. You too have wasted your gifts—by failing to claim them! You too are forgiven though you never knew you needed to be!" *Claim your inheritance! Come home to love!*

PRAYER EXERCISE 4: Meditating with Characters in Luke 15

Open your Bible to the text in Luke 15:11-32, then lay it aside. Spend a few minutes praying in silence to open yourself to anything God may say to you through this ancient parable. Now read the story quietly. Stand and slowly read it a second time, aloud. Then sit down.

●	Meditate on the story, creating an "inner video" of the scenes: the home, the father—and mother—the younger sibling, the older sibling. Now picture the younger one asking for the inheritance, leaving home, then living recklessly in the far country. Go back and visualize the perfectionist young adult still at home laboring dutifully. Picture the father and mother, disgraced and shunned —as they would be by neighbors in Middle Eastern culture, even their business endangered.

●	Now picture the Prodigal "coming to himself," contemplating the return home; then the waiting parent lovingly embracing the returning child. Live into the sounds and smells of the party. Then see the perfectionist sibling as he explodes in anger to the parent. Which character can you identify with most?

●	Spend a few minutes conversing with each: Dialogue with

the Prodigal. Dialogue with the Perfectionist. Dialogue with the father—and perhaps the mother. Let them tell you their feelings and respond with questions and reflections, conversing inwardly or writing in a journal.

● Finally, picture yourself as the resentful, responsible sibling, and hear the word of divine grace to you: "You are always with me, and all that is mine is yours." Begin repeating the words in your mind, slowly, in rhythm to your breathing. Hear it first as *God* assuring you even in difficult times—"You are always with me"— and inviting you to claim your gifts—"and all that is mine is yours." Spend five to ten minutes before continuing.

● Reverse the conversation, slowly repeating the words as *your* prayer to God, with thankfulness that God is always with you: "You are always with me." And offering all your gifts to God: "And all that is mine is yours." Spend another five or ten minutes here. Now take some time to write your reflections on this experience in your journal. Share the experience with a friend or group.

Anger or Apathy: An Invitation

I was always uncomfortable with the stark "time for hate" and "time for war" in the last two lines of the beautiful poem in Ecclesiastes 3. Then it dawned on me. For the exhausted Prodigal who had left home in anger to "feast" on the world, the time finally came for love and peace. And for the burned-out Perfectionist, numbed by years of "fasting" from any intense pleasures, the time finally came to get in touch with his buried feelings. It was a time for war and confrontation with his father whom he would paradoxically now be able to love again! There is "a time for peace," and as Pete Seeger added in his song "Turn! Turn! Turn!"—"I swear it's not too late!"

You may not identify with the extremes of wasteful extravagance or steeled-rage turned explosive. But all of us from time to time know a low-grade boredom or a quiet apathy, the less extreme symptoms of the Prodigal's recklessness or the Perfectionist's resentment.

Our spiritual awakening is beginning when we become aware that we have been trying to mask the emptiness. Whether the emptiness comes from too much of the world or too little of it, *our anxiety is an invitation to live the unlived life.*

PRAYER EXERCISE 5: Space for God

I invite you to become aware of some emptiness in your life: an unfulfilled desire you may rarely express. Gently get in touch with it. One somewhat private person identified the source of her emptiness: "It was that my mother died and never got to see my husband and children. I think of it often." It may be a spiritual "homing instinct"—"a God-shaped vacuum." Once you name it, gently look at ways you may be using to fill it—some good, some not so good. Prayerfully begin to offer the emptiness by thinking of it as "space for God."[13]

Afterward *Some* Are Strong

So the world breaks everyone by one path or another—by too much success or too much failure, by too much feasting on the world or too much self-righteous fasting from it, or a dialectic of both. Maybe you feel like the student who said to me, "I think there is some of *both* the Prodigal and the Perfectionist in me." Then at some point we can begin to see glimpses of the divine Presence *right in the midst of the brokenness*—which is the key to becoming strong in a new sense.

To begin the journey, or begin again, is "to come to oneself"—to recognize that our yearning and the awkward things we do to satisfy it are a kind of clumsy way of praying our way back home, or home again.

We shall not cease from exploration
And the end of all our exploring
Will be to arrive where we started
And know the place for the first time.[14]

Theme 2
Homecomings

CHAPTER III

The Paradoxical Way Home

You have made us for yourself, O God, and our hearts are restless still, until they rest in you.

— Augustine of Hippo

Most of us remember being fascinated by a common theme in fairy tales. A child grows up as an orphan on the street or is banished to survive in the animal world. Then, usually through some circumstances of suffering and surprise, the child discovers that he or she is really the offspring of royalty! As the story is read, or seen on film, we celebrate the homecoming; even adults experience a mini-trance. For a moment our reason is "suspended," and our own orphaned yearning for royal identity is affirmed. We *know* that behind all our experiences of brokenness lies a hidden treasure: "All these examples of wretchedness prove [the human being's] greatness. It is the wretchedness of a great lord, the wretchedness of a deposed king," wrote Blaise Pascal.

The Motivation for Our Re-Turning

Believing begins by trusting in God; its end is trusting that God believes in you: "You are precious in my sight, and honored, and I love you." You begin to taste the love God has for you despite how "wretched" you feel. I had my discouragements over five years working on this project. But once an editor *believed in me,* there was no limit to the energy I put into this manuscript. Love, not fear, motivates us to repentance and new life.

Bill W., one of the founders of Alcoholics Anonymous, used to say that the alcoholic is searching for the Spirit—but went to the wrong address! It is so for all of us. We fill the God-shaped vacuum with some addiction "and our hearts are restless still," to quote Augustine.

Blessed are you if that yearning causes you like the Prodigal to "come to yourself"! This coming to oneself is often the first step in homecoming to God; self-insight through painful learning experiences or psychological counseling may in fact be spiritual insight. "The more conception of God, the more self; the more self, the more conception of God," Kierkegaard wrote.[1]

God can use our human hungers to beckon us home: This is Pascal's first level, the order of "the senses" or Kierkegaard's "pleasure" stage. It is physical hunger that leads Joseph's brothers—perhaps at an unconscious level—to a serendipitous homecoming with their lost brother (Genesis 37-50). Hunger pangs motivate the Prodigal to contemplate home. The sensual sounds and smells of a party cause the Perfectionist finally to uncork his rage and hear the word of grace.

Our restless sinnings can become the birthpangs of our spiritual re-turnings. Reflecting on the traits of midlife—*discontent, restlessness, doubt, despair, and longing*—Anne Morrow Lindbergh said that we would do anything rather than stand still and learn from them: "One tries to cure the signs of growth, to exorcise them, as if they were devils, when really they might be *angels of annunciation*."[2]

Human Passion—Harbinger of Divine Passion

Strangely, the most intense joys often bring about the deepest wounds, and those who have loved us most closely often hurt us most deeply. Jesus was betrayed, even if unwittingly, by a kiss from a close friend. That is why our sexuality—our human capacities for awe and intimacy as well as the sweetness of sexual acts—is a primary expression of our longing to re-turn to God. If our sexuality creates the deepest sensual joy, it also creates the closest beckonings we have in this life to lead us beyond our sensuality to the Joy that is truly lasting. Yet sexual longings may cause our most painful woundings that also lead us back to the Holy. It is a theme of English theologian Charles Williams, and it is woven throughout the novels of Andrew Greeley, John Updike, and others.[3]

The ecstasy and agony of human passion can be the harbinger of divine Passion. Drawing on Dante's unfulfilled love for the young woman he calls "Beatrice," Williams writes that a person will never find what is true unless one has given one's whole heart to that which must ultimately prove false. "All Ye Whom Love or Fortune Hath Betrayed" runs the title of one of John Dowland's seventeenth-century songs. To have loved and lost is to have been prepared to find the Treasure that will never leave us or betray us.

These longings are also manifested when we are addicted to the sweetness of success attached to career. Our sensual desire to achieve may break us, leading us back to our heart's deepest Desire. I have always believed that Dante was right when he said that hell is when God finally gives us what we always wanted! Our addictions would be super-satiated until we would drown in them: There would be no relief from the alcohol, sex, food—or work.

Even though I played it fairly safe in adolescence, I began taking my share of risks in adult life—and getting wounded. Some of these risks have been for the sake of very "spiritual" causes. I can be addicted to my successes, as in the last parish I served. Energized by serving this big historic church—a 1740 "meetinghouse" still used for worship, outreach programs, new members, multiple staff—in times of reckless abandon I was sometimes on a spiritual high. Intoxicated by too many good ideas at once, I have sometimes had more enthusiasm than the institutions and others around me could bear, resulting in painful conflict.

Wounded by too much creativity on my "prodigious" journey, I have frequently "come to myself." In such times I have identified with the venturesome Prodigal more than the older, conservative Perfectionist. I re-turn my gaze homeward to be embraced in the waiting arms of the divine Parent again. At some points in my life there are parts of both the Prodigal and the Perfectionist in me, and I have needed to be born again —and again. "Again" (Greek *anothen*) means "from top to bottom": All my priorities get turned upside down again.

> We are children first
>   then feverishly
>   try to become adults
>   until painfully
> we become children again.
> And again . . .

It is an ongoing "Christian education"—Plato's *education of desire*—spiritual formation around the form of the cross. When we pull back from some of our truly good ideas, others often will pick them up in God's time. No leader receives a greater compliment than when "the folks" finally come up with the leader's own idea. Think of this "pulling back" as spiritual discipline: Sometimes I need to "fast" from some of *my* ideas so they may become *our* ideas. The discipline of self-emptying can save us from depending on a new external crisis to do the emptying.

Two Ways Home: The Worldly Path, the Ethical Path

Both the Prodigal and the Perfectionist in us ultimately come from the same script: *I Did It My Way!* in the words of Frank Sinatra's popular song. Both lead through pain to the cross.

Which is the greater cross, the pain of the Prodigal confronted with emptiness? Or the pain of the Perfectionist confronted with resentment? Neither will change unless confronted by painful circumstances: The Prodigal is confronted by the bankruptcy of material attachments; the Perfectionist by an unfair celebration that called into question his own moral life. The pain is no less for the "moral" person than the "immoral" person. But until they are aware of their pain, both the worldly and the ethical person act the same way: as if they were invincible.

We see this in the drama of *Amadeus*, the budding Mozart (definitely kataphatic!), the "immoral" and prodigal child prodigy. Then there is Salieri who considered himself the "moral" musician of his time, like the older sibling in Luke's gospel. Salieri had made a deal with God: that if he, Salieri, remained faithful and "moral," abstaining from worldly pleasures (definitely the apophatic way!), then God would bless his musical career. And like the perfectionist sibling, Salieri's pain—triggered by Mozart's success—created unquenchable darkness. Both are gifted; both sin; both suffer. Who suffered more? Salieri through his vindictive, self-justifying, relentless inner conflict? Or Mozart living in manic-depressive self-abuse, dying at age thirty-five with only a pauper's funeral? And whose loved ones suffered more? Yet mysteriously the immortal gifts of each were mediated through pain.

The Third Way Home: The Transformative Path

Luther spoke of the "breaking down" process of our homesickness as the "the strange work of love," *opus alienum*. But he was quick to speak of the "building up" process as "the proper work of love," *opus proprium*.

One way or the other "the world breaks everyone"—the alien work. Thank God, the pain caused by either the worldly way *or* the ethical way can lead through the cross to a paradoxical third way, *via transformativa*![4] "So if anyone is in Christ, there is a new creation" (2 Corinthians 5:17). Then "afterward many are strong"—the proper work. It is the transformative way of the Gospel: Old wounds offered to God can become a fresh, creative opening for grace. "Do not be conformed to this world, *but be transformed* by the renewing of your minds, so that you may discern what is the will of God" (Romans 12:2, italics added).

Weakness becomes strength: The tree of death is the tree of life! Worldly adversities can be used to spiritual advantage; obstacles can become opportunities to discern new direction. The risen Lord says, "My grace is sufficient for you, for my power is made perfect in weakness" (2 Corinthians 12:9-10). We see this Christ-life dramatized in the Lord's Supper where the signs of brokenness become the signs of blessing. It is the way of the *paschal mystery* as surrendered wounds and sins become nurturing humus for new life. We can never advance any further in the Christian life beyond this mystery, we can only deepen it.

Like someone climbing a spiral staircase, we may come around to the same issues again and again, *but always at a new level*. My sins may be manifested as self-absorbed perfectionism *or* pleasure, but I am being transformed as often as I lay down the terrible burden of self-importance: "I did it my way." My "world" is no longer the center of the universe.

We do not welcome this change when it comes to us through *the scandal* of the cross—by surprise, by reversal, through some Samaritan person or smarting experience. These are common themes in the stories of Flannery O'Connor.[5] In "Revelation" Ruby Turpin is a good but judgmental person. While sitting in a physician's "waiting" room, Mary Grace, a pudgy "Samaritan" Wellesley student, can feel Ruby's superior attitude. Without warning, Mary Grace hurls a textbook entitled *Human Development* at Ruby. The wound painfully opens "Ruby" to see the "jewel"—the extravagance and inclusiveness of God's grace—a vision of blacks, whites, poor trash, and rich folks, all singing, Glory! Hallelujah!

A Samaritan " . . . had compassion." We have trouble recognizing compassion when it is mediated painfully through a "Samaritan": a body infected with AIDS or a mind affected by Alzheimer's; an estranged family member or an associate who is our fiercest competitor. "Strange work" of love, indeed!

We expect God to speak in the flamboyant: But the Lord was not in the earthquake, not in the wind, not in the fire, but instead in "a sound of sheer silence" (1 Kings 19:11-13)—and not in an answer but a question out of the silence: *What are you doing here?*

"Before praying, relax and rediscover silence," said Origen. Too often it takes a "Jericho road" crisis to silence us and get our attention! So before continuing, I invite you to a time of praying with silence. It is an integral first step to recalling "regenerative experiences," and the most important retreat exercise in this journey.

PRAYER EXERCISE 6: The Sounds of Silence

Group: Do the exercise in the meeting; then take an equal time after-ward to reflect on the experience together. Alone: Find a friend with whom you can reflect later.

Begin by being attentive to any sounds outside; then to sounds inside, if you are indoors. Take several slow, deep breaths—holding the breath for a moment. As you exhale, surrender any conscious or unconscious stress or concerns. Continue this kind of wordless praying. Then in rhythm with your breathing begin to hear the words of Psalm 46:10:

Be still [inhaling, holding]
and know that I am God [exhaling, releasing].

Do not fight distractions, but instead invite them in one at a time, releasing each with the exhaled breath. Listen to the words, "Be still . . . and know. . . . "

Beyond this I will not suggest *how* you should pray in the silence. That will come later. For now, just struggle with it. Abba Arsenius ordered his whole prayer life around this one statement: *Retreat, be still, practice recollection.*

CHAPTER IV

Implosions of Crazy, Holy Grace

*We will always remember the hour, the place and the day when these
seismic shakings of our whole being happened to us. These starry hours
are found throughout our life from earliest infancy. Everyone knows
these moments which have marked them forever. This is not a matter of
"souvenirs," but of the cry of suffocating being within us . . .We must
renew our ties with these awesome experiences, incorporate ourselves to
them, let ourselves relive their particular "quality," relish this taste, this
atmosphere proper to the heart which is our ontological dimension in
which we participate in the divine life.*

—Alphonse and Rachel Goettmann
Prayer of Jesus: Prayer of the Heart[1]

Each of us has filed in our "internal computer" more experiences than we
can consciously articulate at a given moment. The word "is not too hard
for you, nor is it too far away . . . not in heaven or across the sea . . . No,
the word is very near to you; it is in your mouth and in your heart for you
to observe" (Deuteronomy 30:11-14). In Romans 10:5-9 Paul quotes this
text, calling us back to the Torah. The value of a "day of recollection"
lies not in gaining new information but in re-collecting the Word already
within us.

Awakenings: Coming Home on the Journey

These implosions of grace might be called "liminal experiences," somewhere "on the threshold" (Latin *limen*) between our conscious and our
unconscious thoughts. They are "bridgeheads into alien territory" in R.
D. Laing's phrase.[2] In recalling such awakenings, we taste, even if only
for a brief moment, that we are, though not always aware of it, deeply
loved in the core of our being.

Moments of "crazy, holy grace" Frederick Buechner calls them: "Crazy because who ever could have predicted it? . . . And holy because these moments of grace come ultimately from farther away than Oz and deeper down than doom, holy because they heal and hallow. . . . A saving mystery breaks into our time at odd and unforeseeable moments."[3]

W. H. Auden tells how on a June night in 1933 he was sitting on the lawn with three colleagues conversing casually (no alcohol involved, and no sexual interest in each other, he tells us), when unexpectedly something happened. "For the first time in my life, I knew exactly—because I was doing it—what it means to love one's neighbor as oneself." The others were not intimate friends, yet he felt the existence of each to be of infinite value. He experienced flashbacks of past shame, "but the immediate joy was greater than the shame."[4]

John Wesley said of his famous experience at Aldersgate Street Church in London, "My heart was strangely warmed." Martin Luther and John Calvin report such experiences, along with Dante, Julian of Norwich, Pascal, Sojourner Truth, W. H. Auden, Evelyn Underhill, and Simone Weil, Dag Hammarskjold, and Martin Luther King, Jr.

Some experiences are quite ordinary, and they are not always first-time conversions.[5] These implosions of grace have momentarily disclosed the "cry of suffocating being" within us. They are far more common than we think, yet often remain hidden since even our churches do not ecourage their expression. They are not limited to well-known persons, as illustrated by a few brief stories:

● Recently having gone through a painful divorce, Susan confided how a friend visited on New Year's Eve and brought her a single, crystal goblet, "a chalice of love," which she still uses for ordinary orange juice.

● Norman, an unchurched man, was on his way home for lunch. Seeing a "skinny looking minister" crossing the street, he felt sorry for him. Pulling his car over he asked, "Hey, is there anything I can do to help you?" It was the beginning of a life-long ministry with youth.

● Regina had recently recovered from tuberculosis. Serving as a church custodian, she had begun to attend worship but was shocked when the pastor called her name to come forward to be recognized as a church-school teacher—without notice, she claimed. Years later when she told me the story, she had been elected many times as an elder of that church.

● Rose confessed she had been hoping for a dramatic healing for her husband who had Alzheimer's disease. Instead she felt the Presence in an ordinary experience of gentle rain falling on a window pane.

● Never anticipating any extraordinary experience, Bill, a "type-A" business executive, told of a near-death experience, the classic "white light" at the end of a tunnel, an experience profoundly affecting the direction of his life, though he rarely speaks of it.

● A pastor in his sixties revealed that he was from an alcoholic family. He told of the powerful moment when he lost all desire for alcohol—cold turkey—when his preschool son, mispronouncing the word *wine,* asked him, "Daddy, are you drinking *oin* again?"

● Tim, a young adult volunteer in a summer mission project in Chile, told about the gaze of a thirteen-year-old boy, his self-esteem beaten. With head bowed, this boy murmured to his North American visitor, "Good morning, sir." His sad voice, dark face, and downcast eyes are recorded like an icon of the Christ child, a permanent video in his mind's eye, calling Tim to work among the poor.

Psalm 77—Re-Collecting the Scattered Self

Psalm 77:1-10 invites us to reignite the spark of faith by looking over our lives for such simple and profound moments of crazy, holy grace—in times of plain sailing or in times of the dark night of the soul:

1. I cry aloud to God,
   aloud to God that [God] may hear me.
2. In the day of my trouble I seek the Lord;
   in the night my hand is stretched out without wearying;
   my soul refuses to be comforted.
3. I think of God, and I moan;
   I meditate, and my spirit faints. *Selah.*
4. You keep my eyelids from closing;
   I am so troubled that I cannot speak.
5. consider the days of old,
   and remember the years of long ago.

6. commune with my heart in the night;
   I meditate and search my spirit:
7. Will the Lord spurn forever,
   and never again be favorable?
8. Has [divine] steadfast love ceased forever?
   Are [God's] promises at an end for all time?
9. Has God forgotten to be gracious?
   Has [God] in anger shut up
   [divine] compassion? *Selah.*
10. And I say, It is my grief
    that the right hand of the Most High has changed.

Selah is a musical notation calling for a pause, and may also invite the reader to wait and not move too quickly to positive recollections. Verse 10 is a transition, so after a pause the psalmist identifies the cause: "It is my grief." This is *diagnosis.* It is a spiritual grieving—our childish "God" who once seemed power-ful ("the right hand") has changed and now seems power-less to help us.

Then comes the key turning point at verses 11 and 12: This is *prognosis.* "In time of desolation, remember consolations," Ignatius said.

11. I will call to mind the deeds of the Lord;
    I will remember your wonders of old.
12. I will meditate on all your work,
    and muse on your mighty deeds.

By recollecting past awakenings, a powerful Presence becomes available now to awaken us in the dry times. Note the dramatic mood shift in verse 13:

Your way, O God, is holy.
    What God is so great as our God?

In verse 19 the psalmist concludes by recalling the deeds of Yahweh in the Exodus:

Your way was through the sea,
   your path through the waters;
   yet your footprints were unseen.

Implosions of Grace: What Are the Qualities?

In retreat after retreat when folks share these "implosions of grace," I
ask, "What are the characteristics of these experiences? When do they
occur? Do they occur in crisis? In ordinary times? Or both? Are they
programmed or spontaneous?"

I have concluded that they occur in a variety of circumstances, but
they reflect three constant qualities that are congruent with the experiences of saints in the past.

☐ Without exception they happen serendipitously—*in unexpected
circumstances or through unlikely persons*—whether in crisis or time of
tranquility.

☐ There is a *quality of universal love*, a feeling of being loved in
relation to a particular situation or person; yet simultaneously there is a
unitive quality where in the moment one would forgive and embrace the
world.

☐ As a result, invariably at the time and often upon re-collecting
even years later, a person experiences *a change in perspective or
direction*—so that if we pay attention, these provide a living quality of
hope and guidance.

In the moment when Dante saw the young woman Beatrice walking
down the streets of Florence, he was inflamed with love for her, though it
was never reciprocated. In his unfulfilled sexual attraction toward one
person he experienced a state of universal love and charity toward everyone: In that moment he could forgive anyone! Dante takes it a step
further by believing this state to be the way he was always meant to be.[6]
The regenerative experience gave ultimate direction to his life.

Yet these "breakthroughs"—as one friend named them—may result
in little long-term gain unless a person continues with a disciplined
spiritual life. Simone Weil's image of God planting a "seed of love" is
an apt biblical metaphor. These are like a "word from God" planted in

our lives—some on rocky soil with no roots, others among thorns. They hear the word "but the cares of the world, and the lure of wealth, and the desire for other things come in and choke the word, and it yields nothing" (Mark 4:19). What is necessary for the seed to germinate is a *detachment from earthly addictions.*

Yet even after years of lying dormant, when these moments are recollected and named, they still retroactively renew the self and provide direction. Some seed falls on good soil: The "prayer of recollection" is what you do to get your own ground ready again, to paraphrase Kierkegaard. Retroactive grace, I call it.

These awakenings happen while doing menial service, in moments of success or suffering, in crisis or calm, with others or alone while reading a book or contemplating nature, and occasionally during personal prayer or corporate worship—*but always they come unexpectedly.*

● *They may have a mystical quality.* In a time of questioning as a young adult, Lois experienced a persistent feeling as you might occasionally have in a crowd when you become aware of someone looking at you, even though you are not looking at the person. Lois says:

I seemed to hear, "Turn around and you'll see me." Trying unsuccessfully for some weeks to dismiss it and get involved in other things, finally one morning I sat down at the dining room table and said simply, "Okay, God." The Presence that had been behind moved around and stood, smiling, beside me; I turned around, but saw nothing. Yet the Presence was no less real for being unseen. At that moment I knew God was real in a personal way and I knew that God loved me. I felt immersed in a "cloud of love."

● *Or they may come out of very human encounters.* Joyce told me she could not do this exercise; there were no specific times in her life when "God" was real. I knew she had been the first woman ordained to ministry in a conservative denomination. So it occurred to me to ask if she could tell me how she came to be ordained. She told of being at their national church assembly where her "case" was being examined. She was verbally attacked on the sidewalk by two angry delegates accusing her of being insincere, merely wanting to champion a cause. At that very moment a delegate from Joyce's childhood church, the high-school principal of her youth, happened to be walking with her. In a way that was out of character for this quiet now elderly gentleman, he stepped forward to defend Joyce: "How dare you criticize her motivation! I was there when she was baptized! Why, I've known her *since before she was born!*" His word came as a genuine *kairos* moment: a divine affirmation from beyond time like God's word to Jeremiah—through a human "angel."

Compassion: Validating Spiritual Experiences

In biblical terms we are speaking about *repentance* and *faith*, using the metaphors of *homesickness* and *homecoming*. But scripture as well as experience speaks of the need to "test" our spiritual experiences by the fruits of love: "Which of these three, do you think, proved neighbor to the man who fell among the robbers?" An experience proves genuine if it issues in the fruits of love: "The one who showed mercy on him" (Luke 10:36-37 RSV). Alan Paton expressed compassion through his prophetic cry for justice in South Africa, yet he could write to a newly confirmed, young person of the continuing struggle of the journey of faith:

> If you should fall into sin, innocent one, that is
> the way of this pilgrimage;
> Struggle against it, not for one fraction of a moment
> concede its dominion.
> It will occasion you grief and sorrow, it will
> torment you;
> But hate not God, nor turn from [God] in shame or
> self-reproach;
> [God] has seen many such, [God's] compassion is as great as
> [God's] Creation.
> Be tempted and fall and return, return and be tempted
> and fall

A thousand times and a thousand, even to a thousand
thousand.
For out of this tribulation there comes a peace, deep
in the soul and surer than any dream.[7]

Many people have experienced the Presence at points in their lives
but have not moved very far along the transformative path because they
do not stay engaged in the creative disciplines of solidarity, solitude,
study, service, and sense of purpose for being on this earth.

If such experiences of grace come to us by surprise, why do we need
the spiritual disciplines at all? Why go to church? Why get up early or
stay up late to meditate and pray? Why read this book on spiritual disciplines if those are not the likely occasions to experience such reawaken-
ings? A story paraphrased from Anthony DeMello's *One Minute Wisdom* conveys an answer:

"Is there anything I can do to achieve enlightenment?"
"As little as you can do to make the sun rise."
"Then why all these burdensome disciplines you prescribe?"
"Ah! So that you will be awake when the sun rises!"

The first discipline to help keep us awake and get the ground ready
is the fallible, fragile community of believers. It is there that the seed of
love can grow. It is there that these moments can be re-collected, named,
and validated as we begin to move along the way of being re-collected
people.

PRAYER EXERCISE 7:   Recalling Regenerative Experiences

Here is an invitation to read Psalm 77:1-13 (aloud if you are in a
group). Now create your own ending by writing a personal "prayer
of recollection," in silence. Reread verses 11 and 12: *Call to mind
. . . remember . . . meditate . . . muse . . .* Re-collect times, perhaps
long buried, when you experienced a sense that "God's in [God's]
heaven, all's right with the world," to quote Robert Browning—even

in circumstances when your world seemed to be falling apart! They may be quite ordinary, or extraordinary, or some of each. They have the effect of re-collecting the scattered self. (Spend an hour or at least half an hour in silence.)

Prayerfully record some of these in your journal, perhaps creating a special section to record others later as they occur to you. "Harvest" your journal from time to time by coming back and reading them.

Note: This prayer experience is not complete without the sharing as the next psalm [78:1-4] begins with an invitation to storytelling. So to reap the full benefit of this exercise, choose one experience that you are comfortable sharing.

> 2. I will open my mouth in a parable;
>   I will utter dark sayings from of old. . . .
> 4. We will not hide them from their children;
>   we will tell to the coming generation
>   the glorious deeds of the Lord and [Yahweh's] might
>   and the wonders that [God] has done (78:2, 4).

If you are doing this in a group setting, gather in small groups of no more than four. (Or find a spiritual friend or family member, sharing by telephone if you cannot do it in person.) Think of your storytelling and story-listening as "praying"—expressing the heart's deep yearning in God's presence with another person, receiving each other's experience as a gift. Allow twenty minutes for the sharing, five minutes per person.

Join for a few minutes of prayer, silent or perhaps with each saying a "sentence prayer" (a real discipline—*only* a sentence!) giving thanks for experiences shared.

Part II
Training for the Journey

Fruits of Love: What Do You Do after You Say, I Believe?

Theme 3
The Discipline of Community

CHAPTER V

From Believing to Belonging

Share his pain! We must be in this place as one village!

> —Mandinka Elder to Kunta Kinte in the hold
> of the slave ship, in Alex Haley's *Roots*

To rejoice at another person's joy is like being in heaven.

> —Meister Eckhart

Easter stories have the qualities of anonymity, surprise, and short-livedness. Scripture bears witness to our experience of the Presence *incognito*—as a nighttime wrestler, a burning bush, a volcano, water behind a flinty desert rock, a stubborn jackass, sheer silence; as a baby in a cow's feeding trough, a gardener, an advice-giving fisher, a stranger on the road, a guest for supper, the least of these.

These experiences may be logged away, dormant. But recollecting them gives continuity to an otherwise meaningless journey by calling forth the quality of the sacred—the *numinus*, Rudolf Otto called it.

Liminal Experiences: Threshold to Community

"For all thy blessings, known and unknown, remembered and forgotten, we give thee thanks," goes an old prayer. These blessings are often *sub-liminal, under* the threshold of awareness. But like being lost and then catching the faint signal of some distant radio station, once you have heard it, you never really forget it; you know there is something there. You have begun your journey home to God. "Once to have known it, nothing else will do. / All our days are passed awaiting its return," writes Robert Frost.[1]

These *sub*-liminal experiences may contain hidden monsters as well

---

as stars of light: These resurrected gems are bridgeheads into *alien* territory.[2] They call us to union with self, others, and God through two seeming opposites—suffering and joy: The hidden Christ is crucified *and* risen. It is a union illustrated by the words from Meister Eckhart and Alex Haley at the beginning of this chapter: Genuine community involves pain and joy.

☐ In *Roots*, down in the death-dealing hold of the slave ship, a Gambian captive not of Mandinka language like Kunta Kinte screams unintelligibly as the "toubob" whip him. After the captors leave, the clear voice of an elder calls out in Mandinka: "Share his pain! We must be in this place as one village!"[3] Haley once told me this sentence could be the storyline of *Roots*: "Share the pain of all Kuntas! We must be in this place today as one global village!"

You cannot become the new self in isolation. "The more we continue to pray, the less we can avoid getting our feet wet in that ocean of interconnectedness among all persons that flows from the heart of God .... Our suffering acquires the power to span distances," write Barry and Ann Ulinov.[4] And who said it more graphically than John Donne: "No one is an island entire of itself"?

In prayer, we join in Christ's pain: Our "inward groanings" become birthpangs on behalf of the environment as well as humanity (Romans 8:21-23). "All creatures of God's creation that can suffer pain suffered with [Christ]. The sky and the earth failed at the time of Christ's dying because he too was part of nature," wrote Julian of Norwich.

☐ But Meister Eckhart's words form the other side of the paradox, which is just as real: "To rejoice at another person's joy is like being in heaven." There is a quality about these "inside stories" that begs to share the unsharable: "I will open my mouth in a parable; / I will utter dark sayings from of old" (Psalm 78:2, italics added). Only in a community of love is it safe to expose my deepest joys—because some are embedded in my deepest pain.

PRAYER EXERCISE 8: Breathing as Prayer

The wordless language of breathing expresses the three movements of *creation* as we receive the grace of life (inhale); *redemption* as our

blood is cleansed (hold); and the *Pentecost* as we offer ourselves to the Lord of the universe in each moment (exhale): receiving, cleansing, giving. Spend a few minutes "praying" for trees that protect the ozone layer, the rich and poor who breathe the very same air, loved ones near or far. Offer an audible "groan" or "sigh" on behalf of creation or someone in pain (Romans 8:23, 26).

Community: Where We Learn the Language of Faith

Unless these new birthings are named and celebrated, they will atrophy and fail to give direction and meaning to one's life. Put positively, articulating our personal faith experiences in the community of other believers—through words and ritual—takes us into a new dimension, completing our homecomings, continuing to renew them, and enriching the direction they provide.[5] (If you have not completed exercise 7, find a way to tell about one of your "awakenings" now.)

The community of believers is the place where we learn the language of faith, hope, and love. The speech and gestures of worship beckon us to a dance between our woundings at the edge of adventure and experiences of bliss at the still center, a rhythm of journeying and homecoming.

These awakenings quietly prod us to move out from a purely personal believing to belonging. The discipline of community provides the betrothal ceremony where the private *longings* that gave birth to our believing can be wed as our *be-longing* to God—and neighbor.

Language itself creates relationships necessary to sustain human life, as illustrated by a story from the annals of medical literature. In the thirteenth century, Richard of Sicily (Earl of Cornwall) was known for his ruthless experiments on human behavior. Thinking Hebrew to be the divine language that would providentially emerge if children were not "infected" with any other, he isolated a group of infants, instructing their nurse-mothers that these babies were to be exposed to no fondling, no speaking, no singing. Then the chronicler of the "research" states that the shame was Richard's, for the children all died.

Language creates human interaction through symbolic self-expression.

Helen Keller and countless others who do not speak or hear or see demonstrate that life-sustaining communication is not only verbal. The primal gestures of cuddling and holding are the nonverbal language that create the fertile readiness for more highly symbolic language.

The "body language" of affection has been shown to make a measurable difference in the health of drug-addicted babies when volunteers in hospitals have cuddled these isolated children. Holding has therapeutic value *at all ages,* and its absence is related to many childhood problems such as autism and failure to thrive.[6]

Like the primal creation itself, without self-expression a person may remain in deep chaos: "Give sorrow words; the grief that does not speak / Whispers the o'er-fraught heart and bids it break," wrote Shakespeare in *Macbeth.* Without the language of love, we regress into spiritual chaos because "violence is the language of the inarticulate."[7]

But how do we learn the language of unconditional love? "Right speech comes out of silence," wrote Bonhoeffer in *Life Together.* The genesis of the universe is a prototype of the way language shapes our personal lives: "The earth was without form and void" (Genesis 1:2 RSV). Chaos begins to take shape *when the Spirit broods over the abyss, and God speaks*: "Let there be light" (v. 3). Emily Dickinson wrote:

> A Word is dead
> When it is said,
> Some say.
> I say it just
> Begins to live
> That day.

So how do we learn this transforming new language of the Spirit? Training people who would work with Spanish-speaking people in Harlem, Ivan Illich said that if you are going to learn a language, *it is as important to hear the silences in it as it is to know the words.* Often our being silenced prompts our spiritual re-turnings. Like the Prodigal—by a hospitalization, an accident, an experience of death—you "come to yourself."

Ironically and almost too obviously, just as a child learns speech by listening and imitating, we learn the language of faith, hope, and love *by listening, by paying attention*—the meaning of the Hebrew *Shema*. Yet most prayer has been taught as *speaking instead of listening*.

There are three movements in our "listening" as we learn this new language: First—which we have just been doing—we listen to *the call to re-turn* to that deep, unconditional Love. Second, we listen to *the call to celebrate* our first Love—which can happen only in community. Third, in Nietzsche's phrase, we listen to *the call to the "long obedience in the same direction."*[8]

PRAYER EXERCISE 9: Let There Be Light

Find the song "Morning Has Broken" on a recording or in a hymn-book; have it ready to use at the end of the exercise. Read Genesis 1:1-5 silently; then out loud, slowly. Begin to repeat the phrase from verse 3: "Let there be light," over and over, slowly—in rhythm to your breathing. Visualize light breaking into the dark void of creation, then get in touch with some "void spots" in your own life.

● Now gently, as a concern arises, feel the light of Christ speaking to each concern, *Let there be light*. Allow the "distractions" to become intercessions—personal, family, church, world, spiritual, physical, political—one at a time. As each one rises, feel God's re-creative healing Word addressing the concern: *Let there be light*— but it is also the yearning of your heart addressed to God!

● After exhausting all conscious thoughts, continue to hear, *Let there be light.* . . . After a time, let even those words disappear and simply feel yourself as a "new creation in Christ," basking in the light of the Presence. Then, using the hymnbook or recording, pray the words "Morning has broken, like the first morning. . . . "

CHAPTER VI

Shema:
The Language of Celebration

If in your lifetime the only prayer you offer is, Thank You, that would suffice.

—Meister Eckhart

*I have found that the very feeling which has seemed to me
most private, most personal and hence most incomprehensible
by others, has turned out to be an expression
for which there is a resonance in many other people.*

—Carl Rogers, *On Becoming a Person*[1]

"You have forsaken your first love," wrote the angel of the church of Ephesus (Revelation 2:4 NIV). "We love because [God] first loved us" (1 John 4:19). Our listening began with the call to re-turn and contemplate our first Love, the One who says: *You are precious in my sight, and honored, and I love you . . . . You are always with me, and all that is mine is yours.*

Upon our re-turning, the call is urgent: *We have to celebrate and rejoice! This child was dead and is alive again, was lost and is found! Let us eat and make merry!* (Luke 15, adapted).

You are invited to a personal homecoming, yet it is never totally private: "There is no such thing as a solitary Christian," wrote John Wesley.

Be Holy and Whole: Unique Yet At-One-With

The community of believers is made up of once-isolated people who by hearing the Word of their first Love now become a unique people and celebrate the uniqueness of each person in it!

"Hear! [*Listen!*] O Israel, the Lord your God, the Lord is one; and you shall love the Lord your God . . . " (Deuteronomy 6:4 RSV). So begins the formative word for the Hebrew community: the *Shema* [Shemah]—named for the first word: Hear! Listen! It is to be recited every morning and evening in personal and communal prayer: "at home and . . . away, when you lie down and when you rise" (6:7): *Listen, hear, contemplate, discern.* The *Shema* is a call to love God by realizing our own uniqueness *and* at-one-ness, just as God is unique *yet* at-one with all creation.

Shema Yisrael, adonai elohenu, adonai ehad.

[Listen!] O Israel: The Lord our God, the Lord [is] *one* [at-one-with]
(Deuteronomy 6:4 NIV)
[Listen!] O Israel: The Lord [is] our God, the Lord *alone* [unique]
(Deuteronomy 6:4 NRSV)

The two possible ways of translating *ehad* illustrate the wonderful paradox of *singularity and solidarity* so characteristic of the Hebrew scripture. The NIV uses the literal Hebrew word for *ehad*—one. It is a call to love Yahweh by being at-one-with God, self, and all creation: The emphasis is on *integration*—becoming *whole.* The great sin of Western civilization has been its emphasis on "rugged individualism" which all but obliterated the Native American spirituality that preceded us. We desperately need its corrective emphasis on the oneness of the Great Spirit with all creation. For the Hebrew people, "God is the ultimate *with,*" says Jewish scholar Ronald Miller. One might translate the name Yahweh as "the One Who Will Be There" (Exodus 3:14).[2] This with-ness of God is especially significant for Christians because it is fulfilled, the very title for Jesus: "'and they shall name him Emmanuel,' which means 'God-is-with-us'" (Matthew 1:23, see Isaiah 7:14).

But the NRSV is equally valid and calls you to love God by becoming the unique self only you can be: The emphasis is on *individuation*—becoming *holy.* You are "created in the image of God," meaning unique, one of a kind (Genesis 1:26); yet the uniqueness is also manifested in community: "male and female [God] created them" (1:27).

The call to holiness in the Torah and Christian scriptures is a call to become like God—*mimesis*, "mimicking" the divine. Celebrate your one-of-a-kindness: "You shall be holy, for I am holy" (1 Peter 1:16, see Leviticus 19:2 and 20:26): "I have separated you from the other peoples." Kierkegaard spent his life telling us this: *If faith is not deeply individualized, each becoming a distinctive self in Christ, then the community of believers also loses its distinctiveness.* Words from Brian Wren's hymn echo the twin themes:

> God is One, unique and holy,
> Endless dance of love and light . . .
> Everything that is or could be
> Tells God's anguish and delight.
>
> God is Oneness by communion,
> Never single or alone . . .
> Common mind and shared agreement,
> Common loaf and sung shalom.[3]

To be *holy* means to be unique—and at the same time *whole*, at-one-with. The English word *alone* captures this wonderful paradox: *all-one*!

High-Tech, High-Touch: Individuality and Intimacy

Everyone needs time to be "alone" in solitude in order to be "all-one" with community. And every community (even two lovers) needs the compassionate discipline of allowing each member time and space to nurture the self alone, and then come together to celebrate each person's unique experiences. Without the intentional rhythm of aloneness *and* at-one-ment, any community will be fragmented and fractured; its members will not be "all-one"; they will not be "intimate" with each other—even if two physical bodies intertwine sexually!

The Christian community is marked by the call to celebrate and value the distinctiveness of each individual within it. That is the meaning of the celebration of the Prodigal's return: He is accepted for who he is and not required to conform to someone else's ideal personality type. Forgiveness means you are free *not to conform!* This is our third path: "Do not be conformed . . . but be *transformed*" (Romans 12:2, italics added).

Listen! You are unique! No one has had your particular combination of life experiences. *Be the unique self you were meant to be, as God is unique.* Yet to fill our emptiness, we try desperately to copy people instead of God. The great sin of God's people always is to want to "be like other nations" (1 Samuel 8:20).

The expression "high-tech, high-touch" illustrates that people depersonalized by technology are craving both intimacy and individuality. Here is the church's opportunity! Yet the church often copies the culture, leaving no space for us to be vulnerable—to share our hurts and joys—especially in its "showcase to the world," the corporate service of worship, and certainly not in its myriad of task-oriented "committees." I think the Presbyterian translation of Matthew 18:20 is, *Wherever two or three are gathered . . . there form a committee!*

It is good for churches to offer small groups for study and sharing. But in a high-tech world, most people simply do not take time to participate in a "small group" in addition to the basics of Sunday morning and serving on committees in the church and community. After re-collecting our regenerative experiences, this one practice of fostering intentional *koinonia*—relationships with God and others—in every meeting would revolutionize the church by making it a model of community.

PRAYER EXERCISE 10: From Committee to Community

Purpose: To enable "the meeting of persons" in ordinary meetings— in the local church and regional levels. This need take only six to fifteen minutes of the meeting and can facilitate the agenda and improve the decision making!

● **Start using this process with the pastoral staff and boards: They set the tone for the entire church. Large churches need this to keep them caring. First Presbyterian Church, Bethlehem, Pennsylvania—more than three thousand members—has been using an** approach like this for decades.

● Small and average-sized churches need not fear that growth will make them less personal as long as they provide safe places for sharing.

● The paschal mystery of the crucified-risen Christ sets the pattern: Blessing comes out of sharing the brokenness of the world or our lives. "Rejoice with those who rejoice, weep with those who weep" (Romans 12:15).

Process: Pair off in twos—suggesting people meet with "someone you know the least"—and use any questions that promote genuine sharing: (1) What is some *joy* that I have experienced since the group last met? (2) What is some *concern* on my heart right now? (Allow five minutes—two or three minutes per person; leader give a signal at half-way point and again at the end—clap the hands once or ring a soft bell.)

Suggest that each pair spend one minute in *silent prayer*—with eyes closed picturing the face of the partner, lifting up that person's joy with thanksgiving and praying for the concern. Then have partners give each other sign of Christ's peace. *Options*: Offer a "sentence prayer" for each other, still in pairs or with the group as a whole.

Conclude by singing a verse of a hymn or spiritual. Examples: "Spirit of the Living God" or "Kum Ba Yah." The variations for building *koinonia* are endless; use your creativity and humor to create community![4] (For more options that you are free to photocopy, see appendix 2. Also, see exercise 33.)

Worship as Primary Speech: Right-Brain, Left-Brain

The most private feeling in each one of us, if we take the risk to express it, often connects us most deeply with others. You can see how this is true in the lives and works of poets and artists who have dared to express their unique selves. Pure success distances us from others; art that expresses joy silhouetted by human vulnerabilities creates intimacy. The church is to be that place.

Paraphrasing Luther who said that every Christian is a theologian, I say every Christian is an artist! You may think you are unartistic, but the discipline of communal worship is developing the "art"—the unique "being"—that is within each of us. Art is more than just discipline; it becomes "a habit of being." Using Flannery O'Connor's image of art, worship is "something in which the whole personality takes part—the conscious as well as the unconscious mind. I think it is a way of looking at the created world and of using the senses so as to make them find as much meaning as possible in things."5

The discipline of the worshipping community uses all the senses to find meaning in the created world. It is the art of learning prayer as our "primary speech"6—speech that is both left-brain (logical, linear) and right-brain (creative, artistic). In traditional terms, worship employs the verbal language of the Word and the body language of sacramental actions—the Word dramatized.

Language of the Mind: The Word in Context

We listen to the verbal language of the Word—*the Word proclaimed*—loving God with the mind, primarily through methods of "left-brain spirituality" like the reading of scripture, sermon, printed literature, Bible study, and systematic theology. Much of scripture is storytelling which embodies both spheres of the brain. So even the sermon—especially!—and theology are not exclusively linear.

We read words, but how do we give them meaning? This was the question of Philip to the Ethiopian eunuch as he read Isaiah 53, "Do you understand what you are reading?" (Acts 8:30). *Interpretation* is our task in any reading—Homer or T. S. Eliot or the Bible, expressed in the fancy term *hermeneutics*—the science of interpretation. It might better be called *the art of discernment: the art of shema.* It is not just an intellectual task; it is a spiritual one.

Here is a fourfold perspective for *interpreting scripture in its contexts.* (1) We are wisely taught to interpret a scripture passage *in the context of other passages*: Don't take a verse out of context; read what comes before and after it. (2) Read the passage *in its historical context.*

Know what it meant back then before you decide what it means now. Pray to discern what is *timely* from what is *timeless*. (For example, the command not to eat pork in the desert was *timely*: it would mean death. But there is still a *timeless* message: God is concerned how my eating habits affect my total well-being—and the well-being of the planet.) (3) Read the Bible *in its existential context*. God, how are you inviting me? —or challenging me? What is the *new* timely command *for me*? (4) But one more context is important: Interpret the Bible *in the context of the believing community*—living and dead. I can learn from the Word as it "became flesh" in Jerome, Teresa, George Herbert, Evelyn Underhill, Martin Luther King, Jr., or Archbishop Romero. "No prophecy of Scripture is a matter of *one's own [private] interpretation*" (2 Peter 1:20, italics added). Here is a plea for using commentaries, for Bible study in a group, for one-on-one spiritual friendship, for doing theology together, and for personal prayerful reading. The *discipline* of community is to learn from other believers—their gifts and failures. Truly great theologians integrate all of these.[7]

Flannery O'Connor was convinced that anyone left alone with a Bible and inspired by the Holy Spirit is going to be "Catholic" one way or another, even if that person has never heard of the traditional church![8] Sooner or later a person with a genuine spiritual experience will find or create a community of believers.

PRAYER EXERCISE 11: Standing to Read the Gospel

The gospels are written in story form to dramatize and visualize the life of Christ. In churches that invite those who are able to stand for the gospel reading, the act of standing (Greek *anastasis*, "resurrection") is a kind of "body prayer": We rise to meet the risen Christ who joins us in our journey through life's conflicts, joys, and adventures. You may also use this practice in your private devotions. As you stand and read, feel yourself in communion with the risen Christ and with the body of Christ around the world. Suggestion: Stand and read the gospel lesson *aloud*.

Language of the Body:
The Word Dramatized—Ritual, Nature, Music

The apostle Paul invites us to worship with our bodies: "I appeal to you ... to present your bodies as a living sacrifice ... which is your spiritual worship" (Romans 12:1). The *Shema* includes loving God with all one's heart, soul, and *might*—one's physical being. The Psalms offer many examples of praying with the body: folding, lifting, or clapping the hands, climbing steps, bowing, kneeling, dancing, and walking—all recall that the word of Love is enfleshed in one's whole being.

Ritual can be lifeless or incarnational, "embodying" the Gospel. Body language is present as much in the silence of the Quaker meeting or in the lifting of hands in the Pentecostal assembly as in kneeling in a high-church Episcopal liturgy. We need to encourage "at-one-ment" spiritually and ecumenically. "Black folk find white folk afraid of their bodies. Blacks bring their bodies even to worship—especially to worship with."[9]

The two primary signs of this "nonverbal language,"*washing and feeding*, provide the basic paradigm for varied forms involving our senses in worship: "O taste and see that the Lord is good" (Psalm 34:8). As we see, feel, and taste the Mystery, brokenness is transformed to blessing! Calvin compared the sacraments to coloring books for children; so the Creator mercifully provides for sensory experience of divine love for *all* "children" of God.

☐ *The water* of baptism speaks the quality of *resiliency*: Its paradoxical language of *dying* (floods, destruction) and *rising* (renewal, deliverance) reminds us that as often as we are down, Christ rises in us again. As water touches our skin, it is a sign of Christ's cleansing and healing for all kinds of wounds experienced *through our bodies:* A car crash or rape wounds the psyche via the body. Though understood as a one-time experience, baptism may be renewed throughout one's life— with or without using water.

☐ *The bread and cup* of communion speak the quality of *presence through pain:* Through the paradoxical language of *the breaking of the bread*—taking, blessing, breaking, giving—the signs of brokenness become the signs of blessing. One young adult says a high point at communion for him is the *fracture*—the moment when the minister breaks the bread. The "fracture" touches our fractured lives *and* the fractured body of Christ.

Christ's pain is lifted up as a sign of healing for our fractured "body" in its personal, interpersonal, and corporate dimensions. This is right-brain spirituality—dramatic, visual, tactile. We need to feel as well as think. "They devoted themselves to the apostles' teaching and fellowship [*koinonia*, community], to the breaking of bread and the prayers" (Acts 2:42; see theme 6, "The Discipline of Service"). Not only communion but every experience of breaking bread becomes a sacred time.

☐ *The language of the Psalms and music* connect us to community: Psalms are meant to be "sung prayers" of the people of God. You may sing a gospel song in the solitude of a shower or hospital bed; you may sing a chant while driving or alone in a prison cell, but you first learned them through community. So in singing them you are never alone!

Music embodies the form of life itself; through our senses music gives shape to the Mystery at the heart of existence.[10] The origin of jazz illustrates the paschal mystery born out of suffering as white captors deprived African-Americans of their native instruments, acculturating them European style. Voila! Acculturation works both ways. In the safety of their cabins at night, slaves reverted to their native African rhythms, blended with these strange new instruments and meter! The very word *blues* carries the idea of sadness, yet the music can be energizing.

Music can also capture the ecstasy of life, as when we are "enraptured" in a concert: "Music heard so deeply / [that] . . . you are the music / While the music lasts," T. S. Eliot wrote.[11] It is no accident that the Psalms and music married each other: Both contain the capacities for absolute mirth and absolute desolation. "When in our music God is glorified, / And adoration leaves no room for pride, / It is as if the whole creation cried: Alleluia!"[12]

☐ *The wordless language of nature* is also a gentle call to communion: "The heavens are telling the glory of God. . . . / Day to day pours forth speech, / and night to night declares knowledge" (Psalm 19:1-2). Nature is a universal beckoning toward the Divine, *yet without coercion.* The beckonings are subtle, as the psalm continues: "Their voice is not heard; / yet their voice goes out. . . . " Nature's call to re-turn our gaze begins anonymously, love that precedes our consciousness—"prevenient grace."

Corporate Worship: The Vital Nerve

Worship is where prodigals and perfectionists alike can celebrate by naming and claiming our gifts: *You are always with me, and all that is mine is yours.* Then the twin responses of the believer are to celebrate the Gift and to live it out in the world—in the words of the Gospel song, to "trust and obey."

Corporate worship is the vital nerve that nurtures the muscles of personal faith. Then the spiritual muscles can be trained for the "long obedience in the same direction." After the party, the Prodigal was on the road to becoming a Compassionate Parent himself—or a Good Samaritan.

PRAYER EXERCISE 12: Renewing Our Baptism

Here is a meaningful way of remembering our baptism for retreat or congregational settings or as a children's time in worship. Children can understand the common request at home to "wash your hands before coming to the table," to illustrate baptism and communion.

Leader(s), standing: Holding a basin of water, and a towel on your wrist, invite the person next to you to dip his or her hands and place them on his or her own forehead for a moment, perhaps making the sign of the cross, as you speak words such as, "Jay, remember your baptism . . ." (and a few personal words about Christ's cleansing, forgiveness, new life); then the person wipes his or her hands on the towel. Pass the basin and towel to that person, who holds it for the next, and so forth. As this continues, join in singing "There Is a Balm in Gilead," "Amazing Grace," or a children's song. (Allow the option not to participate. This may or may not be followed by communion.)

PRAYER EXERCISE 13: Kneeling—Dying and Rising

Individual or group experience: Read Romans 6:3-4. In baptism, we have been buried with Christ, so that, as Christ was raised, we might walk in newness of life. *If you are able,** in standing position, fold your hands.

Think of some difficult experience, an unreconciled "little death," or a success that may need to be surrendered. As you kneel,* open the hands, letting go of it to God: Visualize yourself while "going down" as dying and being buried with Christ. Stay in the kneeling position a few minutes, eyes closed, letting the mind lie fallow.

While kneeling, you might place your hand on your head with the words: *I am baptized. I am a child of God* (Luther's practice). Or *I am marked as Christ's own, forever (The Book of Common Prayer).*

Now open your eyes and gently rise, picturing the risen Christ rising with you to walk with you throughout the day. Slowly take a few steps, inviting Jesus to walk with you in your journey, visualizing with each step some of the places you expect to be in the day ahead.

In congregational worship: When baptizing an older child or adult, if your church does not practice baptism by immersion, interpret for the people this gesture of kneeling as "dying and rising with Christ" in baptism. Or you might use this exercise as a renewal of baptism, with the *alternatives.

---

* If you are not physically able, you might try an alternative such as raising and lowering the head. Or: Close your eyes and simply visualize yourself standing; then kneeling, leaving some "difficult experience" behind, buried with Christ; then rising to walk in new life.

CHAPTER VII

Shema:
The Language of Paying Attention

Whenever there is a crisis in the church, it is always here: a crisis in contemplation.

—Carlo Carretto, *The God Who Comes*

Attention is the only faculty of the soul which gives us access to God.

—Simone Weil,
on a stamp issued by the French government

Right listening is the source of right behavior. We cannot get away from listening! *Shema* in Hebrew is also the main word for *obey*. In English *obey* is from the Latin *ob-edire* (and its root *audio*) meaning "to listen beneath." Likewise in Greek, *obey* (*hyp-akouein*, root of acoustics) means "to listen beneath." Our highly *audio-video* culture should be experts in *listening* and *behavior*!

Obedience: Listening and Doing

Contemplative prayer is training in "listening from beneath"—to listen beneath the surface, to be attentive, to discern, to empty ourselves of our own prejudiced agenda. This kind of praying is training in holiness *and* wholeness.

"*Listen carefully* to the voice of the Lord your God, *and do what is right* in [God's] sight, and give heed to [God's] commandments . . . for I am the Lord who heals you" (Exodus 15:26, italics added). We are meant to listen through *the words* of Scripture *to the voice* of the Lord: *What are you trying to say to me now, God?* Let me *listen*. Then comes the ethical question of discernment: God, what is the *best* choice for me to make here?

PRAYER EXERCISE 14: Contemplative Healing Prayer

I invite you to spend several minutes simply hearing the words, "For
I am the Lord who heals you" (Exodus 15:26), re-collecting particular times of fragmentation in your life. Before, during, and after each
recollection repeat in the heart again, "For I am the Lord who heals
you."

Listening: Obedience as Attentiveness

"Listen . . . and do." Pay attention . . . then act. Notice what you see,
and then you will do right. This is why simply noticing is so important
for discerning the right action: Notice what your child wore to school
today. Notice the eyes of the person talking to you. Notice the smell in
the nursing home. Pay attention to the number of minorities at your favorite leisure spot. Pay attention to the ache in your shoulder this afternoon. Pay attention to the number of single mothers at the PTA meeting.
Pay attention to the excitement in your spouse's voice tonight.

And once you notice, pray the young Samuel's prayer for discernment. In the wistful story of the boy Samuel, awakened three times from
sleep in "the house of the Lord" at Shiloh, *shema* becomes his prayer:
"Speak, Lord, for your servant is listening" (1 Samuel 3:9-10).

It is a good prayer for any time and place, but it is always my prayer
after a vivid dream. I call it praying your dreams: "Lord, if there's anything you want to say to me in this, I'm listening." Even sleep will not
get in the way of such attentiveness, and it is especially important to have
a spiritual guide if you want to begin listening to your dreams. Not
surprisingly, the old priest Eli, sleeping nearby, was just such a spiritual
companion for the young Samuel.

Two forms of guidance assist our listening to the voice of the Lord:
The first is spiritual companionship; the second is the living traditions of
the community: the Ten Commandments, the Lord's Prayer, and the
creeds.

Guides for Our Journey: Spiritual Companionship— One-on-One, in Families, Committees, Support Groups

We may still speak of *my* spiritual journey, but it is becoming *our* journey. Spiritual friendship is an ancient form of communal guidance and prayer support. It may take the form of finding another person as a *spiritual companion* with whom you can listen for the promptings of the Spirit, formally or informally; and it may also take the form of family prayer and sharing or a small support group.

Spiritual friendship with another believer is one of the neglected disciplines of community that can nurture our attentiveness. Thomas Hart defines it well as *The Art of Christian Listening.*[1] "Soul friends"— *anmchara,* the Irish call it. Spiritual companionship is also service: "The first service that one owes to others in the fellowship consists in listening to them," wrote Bonhoeffer.[2] The more formalized ministry of "spiritual direction" basically consists of one person listening together with another for the "inner direction" of the Holy Spirit.[3] Sometimes, this ministry has been carried on by letters, as with Bonhoeffer's letters from prison to Eberhard Bethge.[4] In a large church in Houston, Texas, Charlie Shedd instituted a program of "prayer partner" (a spiritual friend assigned to each new member who joined).

There are two simple ways that spiritual friendship can be deepened *through existing structures.* One is through the home; the other is through the existing committees and groups in every church. A third way is to develop new, intentional, small support groups.

☐ *The home and family* provide a form of ready-made but neglected small group. The following rituals are applicable for parent (or any adult friend) and child. This might be used by grandparents whose formative role is acknowledged by many young adults, as my African-American friends especially have taught me. Note the importance of a grandmother in the life of the young minister Timothy (2 Timothy 1:5).

PRAYER EXERCISE 15: Share and Prayer with a Child

This exercise uses two basic questions: (1) What is something good happening in your life now (or in our relationship)? (2) What is something that has you a little bit anxious or concerned (or something you would like to see changed)? The adult should take a turn, also answering the questions; then both pray together, silently or aloud. In the prayer repeat the each other's joys and concerns, offering them to God. (This can also be an enriching ritual for couples.)

PRAYER EXERCISE 16: Alternative Graces at the Table

• *Prayerful meditating on food* is genuine "grace" before (and during) meals and may trigger our concern for hungry people. *Leader*: With your eyes open, become aware of your unity with others: Smell . . . see . . . and contemplate the food in front of you, planted by farmers, picked by the poor migrant farm laborers, transported by truckers or pilots. Eyes open, gently lift your hands as intercession on their behalf and as thanksgiving.

• *The most interesting thing:* Charlie Shedd, through his *Fun Family Forum* cassettes, leavened our family table conversation for years to come by the simple suggestion of sharing "the most interesting thing": *In the last twenty-four hours, what is the most interesting thing that happened to each person at the table?*

• *Lighting a candle at the table:* As our children have grown and we all travel more, we are enriched by another simple discipline of community, suggested by Robert Boyer in *Finding God at Home.*[5] Try lighting a candle for each absent family member, for a grandparent who is not present, or for a friend, with a prayer that the light of Christ be with the person(s). Idea: Choose a certain night of every week to pray for a particular person.

☐ *Existing committee meetings* are a ready-made structure to nurture spiritual friendship. I hear people complain, "There are no small groups in our church!" Yet dozens of "meetings" are listed in their parish calendar! "Leaven" these meetings so they become *Church Meetings That Matter,* to use Philip Anderson's title![6] That is the goal of exercise 10, "From Committee to Community," and appendix 2.

☐ *An intentional support group* of people with similar vocational, personal, or family struggles is another form of spiritual friendship. For twenty-five years, everywhere I have lived I either found or founded a colleague support group. I owe my survival, growth, and many friendships to those groups. Ministers preach community but are reluctant to bare their souls to colleagues. Yet vulnerability is our greatest strength: No more powerful form of community exists than twelve-step groups such as Alcoholics Anonymous built on this principle. In caring for a family member with disability, in seeking vocational guidance, in dealing with addictions, a group gives a perspective no individual can give.

"Mainstream" churches are missing the boat when it comes to small groups that attract young adults to more evangelical churches. The *discipline* of community is a call to quit complaining and begin listening to Christ in and through one another, to baptize the existing "meetings" in our churches and homes, and to start new groups to become genuine sources for *the meeting of persons.*

Guides for Our Journey:
The Decalog, The Lord's Prayer, Confessions

For centuries, the Ten Commandments, the Lord's Prayer, and the confessions of faith—or creeds—have been primary communal guides in learning the language of faith, included in nearly every Protestant or Catholic catechism to guide our listening and doing. They are communal: The first two are written *in the plural*—and the very purpose of a creed is to express *the community's language of faith* in worship.

☐ *The decalog.* Literally "the ten word," the decalog simply begins by affirming the *Shema:* Listen first as God speaks (Exodus 20:1)— before you *do* anything. One first listens to "the foreword," which reaffirms God's gracious Word of liberating love: "I am the Lord your God, who brought you out of the land of Egypt, out of the house of slavery" (Exodus 20:2). It is a call to listen, to meditate on "our first love" through recalling personal and communal experiences of liberation. Only then can we listen to—obey—these "Ground Rules for Liberated People." (Return to exercise 7 to recall some of your own "deliverances.")

The essence is in the first and last commands: "You shall have no other Gods before me. . . . You shall not covet" (Exodus 20:3, 17). In the words of the *Shema*: "The Lord is our God, the Lord alone." So *let God be God. . . . And become the unique self that only you are meant to be!* Then everything in between will fall into place, and you will not need to become a cheap copy of what others are or have. As Shakespeare said in *Hamlet*, "This above all: to thine own self be true, / And it shall follow as the night the day, / Thou shalt not be false to any [one]."

Listen, and celebrate your first love! Obedience will follow. "Love God and do as you please," Augustine said. Our obedience will be only slavish duty of the kind Jesus condemned if it does not follow from contemplation of our first Love.

Sabbath, the fourth command, is the hinge and bridge between love of God and love of neighbor. Sabbath means *shema*. It is a command to cease, to be still, to shut down the computers and listen: Contemplate in silence. Sabbath is a call to *contemplate your first love* (the first four commands);[7] then it is a call to *contemplate how best to manifest that love* toward our neighbor (the final six commands).

☐ *The Lord's Prayer.* In Luke 11:1 the disciples asked, "Lord teach *us* to pray," not, "Teach *me* to pray." The message is clear: We cannot learn the language of faith in isolation! "There is no such thing as *my* bread," Meister Eckhart wrote. The model prayer reminds us that we do not pray alone, even in solitude. The very first word in "the disciples' prayer" (Matthew 6:9-13; Luke 11:1-4) connects us with community: *Our* Father. . . . Give *us* this day our daily bread, forgive *us*, as *we* forgive. . . . Lead *us*. . . . Deliver *us*. Each time you turn to God as your heavenly Parent even for a moment, you can *come only as a child* to be "re-generated"—again and again. And a child never develops in isolation.

This paradox of individuality within community is illustrated by the statues of the French sculptor Rodin. The head and bust portray the unique detail of one particular person, yet the base shades into the raw, unfinished rock of the cosmos. "Your will be done on earth as it is in heaven" is a prayer that the purpose of God may be done in and through my unique life, as well as in peoples and nations and the whole universe.

The Lord's Prayer—or the Disciples' Prayer—is a part of the daily office of many churches, meant to be said in personal or group morning or evening prayer. For years I had no regular time for praying it, sometimes not until the next Lord's Day in church. But then I began to combine spiritual and physical exercises, praying it while doing sit-up exercises for my back. (You can do about seventeen gentle sit-ups, depending on how many "forever and evers" you include!) Since I have been praying this way, the Lord's Prayer has become a real friend.

There is life-changing power in this observation: The petition "deliver us from evil" immediately follows on "forgive us our sins as we forgive those who sin against us." The reason is clear. Our greatest temptation is unforgiveness; the greatest evil we will ever need to be delivered from is the deep consequence of long-term resentment. A great release of positive energy occurs when we let go of ancient grudges that sap our strength. This is one of the great truths of the Joseph story (Genesis 37-50; see exercise 38, "Meditating on Forgiveness").

The words of the Lord's Prayer can be learned at two-and-a-half-years of age: That is how old our daughter was when she stayed with the neighbors who taught her the words when her sister was born! But *the meanings* of the prayer take a lifetime—and that is the point of Luther's words about contemplative prayer in relation to this most common prayer form:

Warm the heart and render praying enjoyable, filled with desire, that is the purpose of "Our Father." But the thoughts of Our Father can be expressed . . . in many other words, in more or fewer words. I myself do not attach myself to words and [habits], rather today this way, tomorrow in another way, all in accordance with how warm and desiring I feel. . . . Frequently when I come to a certain part of Our Father or to a petition, I land in such rich thoughts that I leave behind all set prayers. When such rich, good thoughts arrive, then one should leave the other commandments aside and offer room to those thoughts and *listen in stillness* and for all the world not put up obstructions. For then the Holy Spirit [itself] is preaching and one word from [that] sermon is better than a thousand of our prayers. I have often learned more from one such prayer than I could have received from much reading and writing.[8]

☐ *The creeds, confessions, or affirmations of faith.* These include many in scripture itself;[9] they are an aspect of the "language of the body" of Christ. They are not merely logical; they are *doxo*-logical, a blend of left-brain reasoning and right-brain prayer-pictures of God: *Doxo-logy* literally means "glory word"! Creeds are meant to be shouts of praise to God rather than shouts to one another about who believes the right or wrong way. Bishop John Oxenham put it in poetic theology:

Not what, but Whom I do believe,
    For Christ is more than all the creeds,
    And His full life of gentle deeds
    Shall all the creeds outlive.
Not what do I believe,
    but Whom!

We spend much time articulating and defining the *what* of our faith —creeds and confessions, theology, doctrine, ethics but little time nurturing the *whom*—the relationship to God through prayer. Creed comes from the word *credo*, which means "I believe." Prayer is where our believing gets its guts, its compassion: "And therefore I suffer as I do. But I am not ashamed, for I know whom I have believed," the apostle Paul, or his alias, wrote to the young pastor Timothy (2 Timothy 1:12 RSV). Not *what*, but *whom* I have believed.

To confess takes courage. *Confess* is one of those two-sided biblical words: One side is *confession of sin*, the other is *confession of faith*, dear to those of the Reformation heritage. *Confess*, or its cousin *profess* conveys taking a stand: It takes courage to confess your sin *or* your faith; it makes you stand up and stand out.

So the confessions of the church call us to our unity *and* our uniqueness, which is another way of saying that they assist our training in wholeness *and* holiness. Peter's confession at Caesarea Philippi–"You are the Christ, Son of the Living God!"–is doxological, phrased in the second person as the form of a prayer. It is certainly *not* logical, for Peter clearly did not understand the meaning of his own words!—immediately telling Jesus not to suffer (Matthew 16:13-23). Creeds call us to aspire to more than we understand.

The martyrs and *confessors* are those willing to die for confessing their faith. Jan Hus, a reformer burned at the stake in Bohemia long before Luther and Calvin, died with the "prayer of the heart" on his lips: "O Lord Jesus Christ, Son of God, have mercy on me a sinner" (see exercise 37). In Orthodoxy, the first half of the prayer is understood as confession of faith: *Jesus is Lord and Christ!*

The body of Christ will always be imperfect; naturally its body language and verbal language will be imperfect too! The body of Christ is one, yet diverse. It is holy and yet common; apostolic yet contemporary. Like the bread of communion, it is whole, yet when fractured, it paradoxically transmits healing through its brokenness.

Language is learned in human community. Each of the "official creeds" has a sort of astigmatism. Using this visual metaphor, even with the many "scratches on the lenses" of my old eyeglasses, in an emergency I will pick up an old pair, and they will help me focus enough to get where I need to go. I am the first to confess to the many "scratches on the lenses" of the church's confessions, but they are to help us focus on Christ as the icon of God's love (Colossians 1:15). Someone said our language about God points us to the place on the horizon, beyond which is God. That is what the creeds are meant to do.

PRAYER EXERCISE 17: Praying a Creed

Many churches encourage saying a creed as part of private daily prayer. If that is not your custom, you might want to find a way to incorporate the Jesus Prayer, a biblical confession of faith, and of sin: "O Lord Jesus Christ, Son of God, have mercy on me a sinner."

Instead of *looking at the scratches,* try putting the glasses on and *looking through them!* Try standing, alone, and saying the Apostles'

---

or Nicene Creed or a biblical creed (Deuteronomy 26:5-10, Philippians 2:5-11, or Colossians 1:15-20) *out loud* as an act of praise that says something more about "the Mystery of Christ" than you are able to understand. Become aware that, even alone, you are joined to a global community spanning the centuries.

Speech and Silence: Marks of Community and Solitude

Part of the *discipline* of community is to humble myself to associate with, even submit to, those whom I see as less than perfect witnesses for Christ! "Forgive us our sins as we forgive. . . . " Only the discipline of solitude can balance the imperfect discipline of community: "One does not exist without the other. Right speech comes out of silence, and right silence comes out of speech," wrote Bonhoeffer.[10]

The community is called to *listen before speaking*, as every new-born learns language by listening and imitation. According to the model prayer, says Calvin, we come as "teachable" children—to listen. That is how we learn this new "body language," the corporate speech of the body of Christ. Yet most of Christian prayer has been taught as speaking. To develop methods for "listening prayer" is to cultivate the discipline of solitude.

Theme 4
The Discipline of Solitude

CHAPTER VIII

Sabbath
as Solitude-in-Community

Authentic Christian contemplation transforms contemplatives into
prophets and militants into mystics.

—Secundo Galilea, "Politics and Contemplation"[1]

The gospels were written after the Resurrection in a format like a historical novel to convey that the living Christ accompanies us in our conflicts
and poundings and dazzlings and temptings and beatings and illumin-
ings: Emmanuel, "God is with us!" As they journey "slouching towards
Bethlehem" and flee into Egypt, the holy family's sojourn through pain
and joy is our own: Political oppression, violence against abused mothers and helpless children and fearful fathers . . . can become birthpangs
of our own spiritual re-beginnings. Jesus deliberately chose to join our
human struggle by receiving a sinner's baptism from John (Matthew
3:13-17). And the voice from heaven addresses each of us: *You are my*
beloved [Child]; in you I am well pleased (v. 17). Because the beloved
refers to the beloved community, the One represents the many, and the
blessing is now for all, as the many represent the One.

Immediately after the high point of being baptized, Jesus is led by
the Spirit into the desert to be tested and tempted: When we begin to live
out our baptism, we become vulnerable to evil forces that distort our
original blessing. But by filling every space with constant activity, we
may not even know that we are being pulled off course. There are two
ways of being lost: in the desert with no signposts or in a dense forest,
with too many signposts competing for our souls. We in Western culture
are lost in the "forest," bombarded with competing words. What we
need is not more words but the silence of the desert to clear our vision, to
enable us to listen for the deep Word that is already within us.[2]

Jesus deliberately chooses the desert. In the spirituality of "desert"

---

solitude, we shut down the internal computer long enough to listen to the Word already within us—*You are my beloved child.* This is the ground of our true *being* in Christ, which must be the source for any of our *doing* to be of lasting significance in community. Unless we claim the gift of solitude, we are in danger of the messianic temptations: Our "good ministry" may fill our own unmet needs and put others in an inferior position.

Creative Balancing: The Rhythm of Jesus' Life

Without the discipline of community, solitude degenerates into isolation and self-absorption; without the discipline of solitude, community degenerates into enmeshment and codependency. Just as the human psyche requires a rhythm of sleep and activity, the soul is endangered without the vital balance of retreat and involvement, silence and speech, resting and risking. The Christ of the gospels is both the energy Source and the saving Pattern for this new life.

The gospels portray Jesus' continuing struggle to balance the creative movements of *involvement* with people and *withdrawal* into solitude: "In the morning, while it was still very dark, he got up and went out to a deserted place, and there he prayed. And Simon and his companions hunted for him. When they found him, they said to him, 'Everyone is searching for you'" (Mark 1:35-37). Jesus had been working late into the previous night, spending and being spent, yet even in his early-morning desert space he is interrupted. Our struggle to find solitude *is* Jesus' struggle. Yet the inner clarity of Jesus' mission is born precisely out of *the interrupted solitude:* "for that is what I came out to do" (1:38). Out of solitude our purpose for being on this earth becomes clear.

On their return from the healing mission (Mark 6:7-13), the disciples got devastating news: John the Baptist had been beheaded by Herod (6:14-29). *In the context of our physical exhaustion and grief, Jesus invites us to solitude:*

> Come away to a deserted place all by yourselves and rest a while. For many were coming and going, and they had no leisure even to

eat. And they went away in the boat to a deserted place by them-selves. Now many saw them going and recognized them, and they hurried there on foot from all the towns and arrived ahead of them (Mark 6:30-33).

The risen Lord participates in our struggle to rest and pray.

The effect of this interruption in Jesus' solitude is *not irritation but compassion*: "As he went ashore, he saw a great crowd; and he had com-passion for them, for they were like sheep without a shepherd" (6:34). Prayer is not so much a quantity of time as an intent of the heart. If the heart is deliberately struggling to set aside time alone with God, *then compassion will be its fruit,* regardless of the interruptions, regardless of whether one actually achieves the goal of solitude.

It is out of an experience of solitude in prayer that Jesus made *the decisive choice to surround himself with community:* "He went out to the mountain to pray; and he spent the night in prayer to God. And when day came, he called the disciples and chose twelve of them, whom he also named apostles" (Luke 6:12-13). Luke the Physician wants us to experience a continuing healthy rhythm in our ministry with Jesus: "But he *would withdraw* to deserted places and pray" (Luke 5:16); the Greek verb implies a continuous, repeated activity.

PRAYER EXERCISE 18: Praying with Slaves and a Martyr

Group or individual experience: **First, find a hymnbook with the African-American spiritual "Steal Away to Jesus." Open to the hymn and set it aside. Or you may simply use the lyrics below. Prayerfully read aloud:**

Dietrich Bonhoeffer is remembered as a twentieth-century martyr. Yet his lonely personal life, courageously lived in a Nazi death camp protesting the holocaust, was sustained by a life of rich solitude in community. Bonhoeffer had required the students in the 'underground seminary' to spend at least a half an hour daily meditating and praying with Scripture—in addition to their theological study of the Bible.[3] In his timeless book Life Together, *Bonhoeffer continues to speak eloquently of the vital balancing of the Christian life:*

Let [the one] who cannot be alone beware of community. [One] will only do harm to [oneself] and to the community. Alone you stood before God when God called you; alone you had to answer that call; alone you had to struggle and pray; and alone you will die and give an account to God. You cannot escape from yourself; for God has singled you out.... If you refuse to be alone you are rejecting Christ's call to you, and you can have no part in the community of those who are called.

But the reverse is also true: Let [the one] who is not in community beware of being alone. Into the community you were called, the call was not meant for you alone. In the community of the called you bear your cross, you struggle, you pray. You are not alone, even in death, and on the Last Day you will be only one member of the great congregation of Jesus Christ.... If you scorn the fellowship of the [brothers and sisters], you reject the call of Jesus Christ, and thus your solitude can only be hurtful to you.... Only in the fellowship do we learn to be rightly alone and only in aloneness do we learn to live rightly in the fellowship. It is not as though one preceded the other; both begin at the same time, namely, with the call of Jesus Christ.[4]

Now begin to sing (or say) this beautiful spiritual, *a cappella:*

Steal away, steal away, steal away to Jesus.
Steal away, steal away home. I ain't got long to stay here.
My Lord, God calls me, God calls me by the thunder!
The trumpet sounds within-a my soul:
    I ain't got long to stay here.

If you are in a group, ask them to hum *the first two lines* as the leader begins to speak [if alone, hum in your mind as you read]:

Picture African slaves in the cotton fields singing these words, working in solitude, separated geographically from one another, yet in a community of the Spirit, united by suffering and hope, stealing away in their hearts to Jesus for spiritual freedom, and stealing away in their minds with Sojourner Truth to political freedom.

Then conclude by singing the first two lines again, followed by a holy silence.

Solitude and Sabbath: A Prophetic Edge

"Steal Away" is a profound example of the unity of personal and political liberation, earthly survival and eternal hope, solitude within community. It is "subversive prayer" in the best sense of that expression: Contemplation that might seem to rob time from action, actually creates a more powerful kind of action. Prayer *sub-verts* our agenda, turns it upside down.

The contemplative life brands the believing community as different: It is counter-cultural to value silence over speech, spiritual re-creativity over economic productivity. It has been said down through the centuries that it was not so much that the Jews preserved the sabbath as that the sabbath preserved the Jews! In agrarian society, the sabbath served as a kind of religiously legislated labor union, protecting not only men, but women, children, even slaves and beasts of burden from the dangers of primeval workaholism. Growing up on a farm, I can attest to the bliss with which we looked forward to "a day of rest and gladness" that owed its direct roots to the Hebrew sabbath. If we lose the discipline of solitude, we endanger our spiritual uniqueness. The crisis of the church is a crisis of contemplation.

Sabbath is like T. S. Eliot's "still point of the turning world."[5] *Yet sabbath is not identical with solitude;* it has elements of all five spiritual disciplines (see **image 1**). Sabbath includes communal celebration as well as personal solitude. It contains elements of learning as well as service, which Jesus dramatically illustrated by teaching and healing on the sabbath. Out of sabbath contemplation comes a deep sense of purpose for life: vocation.

From the perspective of our "wheel" (*illustrated on the following page*), one experiences dimensions of "home" in all five spheres, just as

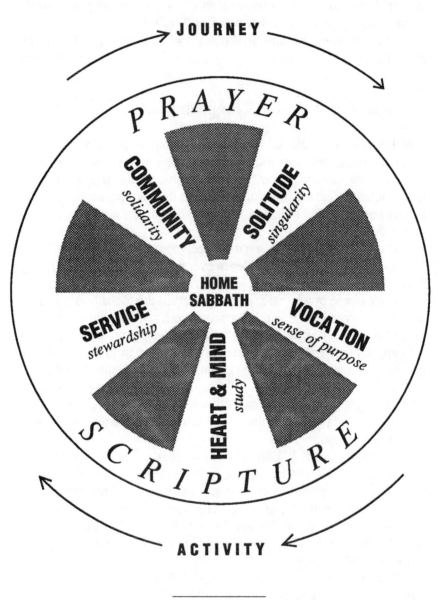

Image 1

The Alban Institute

in Hebrew tradition sabbath includes dimensions of communal liturgy, study, and hospitality, as well as personal solitude. In the same way, scripture and prayer are not isolated disciplines; they form the rim of the wheel, permeating and unifying all five areas. The Word becomes flesh in all of life: in corporate and private prayer, in study and serving, and discerning our purpose on this earth.

The goal of *sabbath time*[6] is to make us *prayerful, playful, and passionate* in all spheres of life. As Mark's gospel said of Jesus: "Come away . . . and rest a while. . . . And they went away *on a boat*. . . . And he had *compassion* on [the crowd]."

Sabbath time spent in contemplation gives us the courage not to sell out to the world's standards, courage to discern when we are called to be priestly and how we are called to be prophetic. Authentic sabbath transforms militants into mystics and mystics into prophets.

To live this radical life of solitude-in-community is to live *off balance*. In a Flannery O'Connor story, the Misfit says, "Jesus was the only One that ever raised the dead, and He shouldn't have done it. He thrown everything off balance. If He did what He said, then it's nothing for you to do but throw away everything and follow Him."[7] The radical celebration for the wayward Prodigal throws life "off balance" for the religious Perfectionist. We can only adapt to this new life if it becomes a dance, between the center and the edge, between resting and risking, between the security of home and the frontier of adventure.

But to follow the analogy further, the purpose of the *discipline* of claiming sabbath is to train yourself so that right while you are on the active journey, just in a moment's turning to God, the edge itself becomes the center: The circle moves to embrace you, and you are home again even while out on the edge.

ASSESSMENT EXERCISE

Take a few minutes now to do a spiritual self-assessment, using appendix 1, "Goals for Spiritual Disciplines" and image 1. Note and pray for the area(s) where you desire to grow: Assess the "rim" of your life (scripture and prayer) as well as the "spokes." This tool

may also be used as a means of renewing your congregation and as a means to evaluate and plan goals for your church. (Permission is given to duplicate appendix 1 and image 1 for use within your church or group.)

Rooted and Grounded in Love: Underground Prayer

The fruit-bearing tree of life is a prolific biblical metaphor. "I pray that . . . you may be strengthened in your inner being with power through [God's] Spirit, and that Christ may dwell in your hearts through faith, as you are being rooted and grounded in love" (Ephesians 3:16-17). "I am the vine, you are the branches. Those who abide in me and I in them bear much fruit" (John 15:5). "Their delight is in the law of the Lord, / and on [God's] law they meditate day and night. / They are like trees planted by streams of water, / which yield their fruit in its season" (Psalm 1:2-3).

Yet it is not so simple that the roots nurture the tree; the vital feeding takes place *in the interaction* between the secluded root system and the visible tree above ground, in the process of photosynthesis. This is a parable of the underground life of prayer that nurtures us through the interaction with our active, visible life in the world. If you look at the profile of a tree (**image 2**), what you *see* is only what is above ground. *Shema* (the trunk) points both ways: Attentiveness to God in underground prayer makes us more attentive to the world's need.

Image 2

The tree, seen from above (**image 3**), looks similar to the wheel. The branches, circular, moving, reach out toward the world yet connect to the trunk in the still point of the center, going deep down into the darkness of silence.

These nurturing elements are absorbed over time in quiet darkness. One of the greatest barriers to authentic listening to the "still, small voice" is our Western mindset that prayer must have some immediate, tangible result, as if God were "the God of the machine." In the Bible the primary metaphors for praying are not *speaking* or *doing,* but *abiding, waiting, watching, listening,* and *silencing, in the dark as well as in the light.*

Image 3

The Alban Institute

CHAPTER IX

Solitude and the Night of the Soul

The soul has to go on loving in the emptiness, or at least go on wanting to love, though it may only be with an infinitesimal part of itself. Then, one day, God will come to show [Godself] to this soul and to reveal the beauty of the world to it.

—Simone Weil, *Waiting for God*

Silence and activity are not so neatly balanced: One break-out root, wounded by an obstacle, can supply more elements than many "normal" tree roots. We never welcome the obstacle. Yet one of the most common experiences for Christians is the times of dark discouragement like that of Job: "O that I might have my request, / and that God would grant my desire, / that it would please God to crush me, / that [God] would let loose [the divine] hand and cut me off! / This would be my consolation; / I would even exult in unrelenting pain" (Job 6:8-10).

When we undergo such experiences, other Christians sometimes react like "the comforters of Job," treating us as if we had completely lost the faith. At such times one may only be able to pray: "I believe; help my unbelief" (Mark 9:24).

PRAYER EXERCISE 19: I Believe, Help My Unbelief

Read Mark 9:14-29. Focus on verse 24, where the father cries out to Jesus on behalf of his disabled child. Open a journal to two blank pages. On the top of the left page, write as a prayer, *I believe.* On the right page, *Help my unbelief.* On the left list prayerfully what you *can* believe and affirm. On the second page list doubts or barriers to believing, *and outgrown beliefs.* For example, *I don't believe* that God causes cancer. *But I do believe* that Christ feels the pain of my friend _____ who has cancer and the pain of her family.

The Dark Night: Anxiety versus Creative Purging

The dark night of the soul is a time of purification and purging. Often childhood images of God are shed so that a more genuine faith can be born. It is a sort of this-worldly purgatory, "to suffer various trials, so that the genuineness of your faith—being more precious than gold that . . . is tested by fire" may be revealed (1 Peter 1:6-7).

> Out of the depths I cry to you, O Lord.
>> Lord, hear my voice! . . .
> My soul waits for the Lord
>> more than those who watch for the morning,
>> more than those who watch for the morning (Psalm 130:1-2, 6).

In the old prayer books, Psalm 130 used to be listed by its first two words in Latin, *De Profundis*: "From the depths" God may bring something truly *profound*. Such a time may or may not be related to an outward crisis of loss. But it becomes a time for deep trusting in that "underground prayer" where the roots may be wintering in preparation for new growth. The Psalms are full of such experiences: "In the day of my trouble I seek the Lord; / in the night my hand is stretched out without wearying; / my soul refuses to be comforted" (77:2).

The Spanish mystic John of the Cross lived by the words of Psalm 139, coming back to them again and again:

> If I say, "Surely the darkness shall cover me,
>> and the light around me become night,"
> even the darkness is not dark to you;
>> the night is as bright as the day,
>> for darkness is as light to you (vv. 11-12).

☐ *One unhealthful response to the dark night is to look for God in the wrong places.* We naturally expect God in the beauty of stained glass, organ chorales, sermons, poetry, prayers, scripture. Instead we may need to enter the dark emptiness. In an old vaudeville act, a lone man would come out onto a stage, surrounded by a single shaft of light from a street light, head bowed, obviously looking for something. A lone policeman would join him in his search:

"What are you looking for?"

"Oh, the key to my house."

They continue to look, unsuccessfully.

"Are you sure you lost it here?"

"Oh no, over there."

"Then why in heaven's name are you looking for it here?"

"Oh, because there's no light over there!"

True, God is sometimes in our experiences of beauty. But beauty is given to sensitize us to see the suffering Christ in "the least of these"—the unlikely faces of the poor, the sick, the dying, the oppressed—or in the poverty of our own dark night. To see beauty in the unpredictable requires patient waiting for the sun to rise.

☐ *Another unhealthful response is impatience, wanting to go through the dark night quickly.* Sometimes psychotherapy may help us spiritually. And there are many how-to books on spirituality. *But no one should try to remedy the dark night for us*—if that is truly what we are experiencing. When a butterfly is about to break out of the chrysalis and unfold its wings, the struggle looks very painful. It seems to take forever. If you watch, it would be tempting to take a pair of scissors and give it a merciful snip. But if you do, it will never fly but will walk around with a distended body and live only a short time. The "merciful snip"—meant to "fix" its pain—is not merciful at all. *It is in the struggle* to come out of the cocoon that the no-longer-useful fluid is expelled, so that a leaner creature can then be airborne. No one can "do the struggle" for the butterfly. No one can do the struggle for us.

We could wish to have such a struggle only once in our lives and be done with it, but it happens to some more often than others, and in emotionally deeper ways to some. I take great courage from the painful experiences of the psalmists, Julian, Luther, John of the Cross, Kierkegaard, Howard Thurman, Evelyn Underhill. All serve as "guides in the desert" for us. Another is Simone Weil: Born Jewish, she had never read any mystical works. Yet in the midst of suffering and in spite of great doubts, she writes that "Christ himself came down and took possession of me." In her short life (1909-43) her "dark night" combined intense personal suffering, brilliant intellect, mystical prayer, and concern for the poor.

> Affliction makes God appear to be absent for a time, more absent than a dead [person], more absent than light in the utter darkness of a cell. A kind of horror submerges the whole soul. During this absence there is nothing to love. What is terrible is that if, in the darkness where there is nothing to love, the soul ceases to love, God's absence becomes final. The soul has to go on loving in the emptiness, or at least go on wanting to love, though it may only be with an infinitesimal part of itself. Then, one day, God will come to show [Godself] to this soul and to reveal the beauty of the world to it, as in the case of Job.[1]

I have spoken here of the "dark night" *before* addressing "methods" of prayer (the next chapter), because all the methods in the world cannot replace the value of one's unique struggle of the soul. The one way of praying that may prove to be most helpful may seem like no praying at all. It is like that of Elijah finding that God is *not* in the dramatic, the earthquake, wind, or fire, but rather in *the sound of sheer silence* (1 Kings 19:12).

Beyond the Dark Night

In *O Blessed Night* Francis Nemeck and Marie Theresa Coombs treat the dark night in relation to recovery from addiction, codependency, and attachment. Biblically, *darkness* (Hebrew *hoshek*; Greek *skotos*) connotes destruction, dread, and disease; whereas *night* (Hebrew *layil*; Greek *nux*) embodies mystery, knowledge, and transformation.[2] *The Mystery of Christ transforms destructive darkness into a night of beauty.*

A student told of asking a therapist the difference between depression and the dark night. The counselor paused, then answered: the outcome. Beyond the depths of Psalm 130, on the other side of the dark night, we find in Psalm 131 a new relationship with God, the image of a weaned child, a tempered spirituality, leveled of perfectionism and codependency:

O Lord, my heart is not lifted up,
>my eyes are not raised too high;
I do not occupy myself with things
>too great and too marvelous for me.
But I have calmed and quieted my soul,
>like a weaned child with its mother;
>my soul is like a weaned child that is with me (vv. 1-2).

Kenosis: The Art of Daily Self-Emptying

"Relying on God has to begin all over again every day, as if nothing had yet been done," wrote C. S. Lewis. By the art of daily self-emptying we enter a bit of the darkness, "leveling" our enthusiasms and preparing for future struggles. Yet many do not know how to begin all over again or question the value of "emptying prayer" with no particular thought or task.

The V-shaped diagram titled *Kenosis* (**image 4**) illustrates the "self-emptying" pattern of the incarnation described in Philippians 2:5-11:

Let the same mind be in you that was in Christ Jesus,
who, though he was in the form of God,
>did not count equality with God
>as something to be exploited,
but emptied himself,
>taking the form of a slave,
>being born in human likeness.
And being found in human form,
>he humbled himself
>and became obedient to the point to death—
>even death on a cross.
[Then comes *pleroma*, fulfillment, the other side of the paradox.]
Therefore God also highly exalted him
>and gave him the name
>that is above every name,
so that at the name of Jesus

every knee should bend,
in heaven and on earth and under the earth,
and every tongue should confess
that Jesus Christ is Lord,
to the glory of God the Father.

"Have *the same mind.*" Christ's self-emptying is the model for education, our "spiritual formation" (see theme 5, "The Discipline of the Heart and Mind"). It is the paschal mystery: The seed "disintegrates" alone in the still, dark soil only to be "exalted," to germinate and bear fruit in community.

The idea of emptying the mind runs counter to our normal way of thinking and praying: It begins by "listening" instead of "talking." Yet "emptying" is not just something from Eastern religions, and the goal is not to *stay in a passive state*, but to move from willfulness *through passivity* to willingness where our actions have a new quality. It is thoroughly biblical, echoed here in this "hymn-creed" of the early church at Philippi. It is a new kind of knowing: "Be still, and know . . . " (Psalm 46:10).

Kenosis is when the Prodigal "came to himself." *Kenosis* is intentional sabbath that empties my prescribed agenda. *Kenosis* is the Christ-life that gives balance to my life: "Yet not what I want but what you want" (Matthew 26:39).

Kenosis is a thoroughly "evangelical" concept, as English nonconformist Richard Baxter gives the "prescription," "Get thy heart as clear from the world as thou canst. Wholly lay by the thoughts of thy business, troubles, enjoyments, and everything that may take up any room in thy heart. *Get it as empty as thou possibly canst,* that it may be more capable of being filled with God."

I invite you to take ten minutes for prayer in simple silence, going back to exercise 6. Try to incorporate *at least five to ten minutes of silence each day*, as part of at least half an hour of set-aside prayer time.

KENOSIS—SELF-EMPTYING

"Let the same mind be in you that was in Christ Jesus, who, though he was in the form of God, did not regard equality with God as something to be exploited, but emptied himself, taking on the form of a [servant], being born in human likeness. And being found in human form, he humbled himself and became obedient to the point of death—even death on a cross. Therefore God has highly exalted him..." (Philippians 2:5-9).

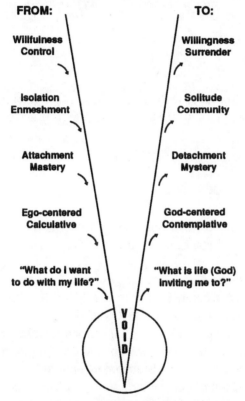

FROM:

Willfulness
Control

Isolation
Enmeshment

Attachment
Mastery

Ego-centered
Calculative

"What do I want
to do with my life?"

TO:

Willingness
Surrender

Solitude
Community

Detachment
Mystery

God-centered
Contemplative

"What is life (God)
inviting me to?"

VOID

"Those who want to save their life will lose it,
and those who lose their life for my sake...will save it." (Mark 8:35)

"Unless a grain of wheat falls into the ground and dies,
it remains alone; but if it dies, it bears much fruit." (John 12:24 RSV).

Adapted from an anonymous source, 1992.
Kent I. Groff and Sanford Alwine, Oasis Ministries for Spiritual Development, Inc.

Image 4

CHAPTER X

Barriers, Benefits, and Bridges

*There is a great difference between the skill and the grace of prayer.
The skill consists chiefly in a readiness of thought consistent with the
various aspects of prayer. . . . The grace consists in the inward workings
of the heart and conscience toward God and our life of faith.*

—Isaac Watts

We all set goals for prayer with good intentions and then think we fail.
But actually we cannot fail; the struggle to pray *is* praying! So keep on
praying!

Claiming Solitude: The Barriers

Our goal is not to lay claim to solitude but rather to let God claim us.
But no one will hand you time to pray: You have to *steal* some time to
steel yourself!

☐ People usually start by naming *external barriers*, the telephone, a
barking dog, etc. A woman, for instance, said she lived on a noisy corner
where trucks went by constantly. A young adult in the group suggested
she might get a "walkperson" and, using earphones, play quiet music as
background. But not all outer distractions have solutions and coping
with them can make our prayer life more meaningful.

☐ Then there are *physical distractions, such as sleep.* Consider
Peter's vision in Acts 10: "About noon . . . as they were on their journey
. . . Peter went up to the roof *to pray*" (v. 9). In his hunger, Peter fell
asleep, dreamed of a sleep symbol (a sheet) and a hunger symbol (clean
and unclean foods). Peter's sensual, kataphatic, imaging prayer became
the watershed of the early church to take the Gospel to the Gentiles. As
long as the intent of the heart is *to pray*, none of our distractions, hunger,
sexual urges, sleep, mind-wandering, can thwart God purposes. You

may find help by *inviting* the distractions into your prayer instead of *fighting* them (see exercises 6, 9, and 38).

☐ But the far deeper barriers are *the inner distractions.* People mention lack of discipline, but behind this other demons often lurk. Some unforgiveness creates a block. We doubt the validity of prayer itself, especially intercessory prayer; it seems like a waste of time. "Nothing happens" in silence—or if it does we question our own sanity! (I like Lily Tomlin's quip, "Why is it when we talk to God, we're said to be praying, but when God talks to us we're said to be schizophrenic?") The deepest inner barrier to solitude is that aloneness reminds us of our fear of death itself. So we avoid it.

But it is best simply to begin with the barriers we are aware of and deal with them. A pastor confided, "I'm not sure if prayer really makes any difference." Her church held prayer vigils at the time of the Persian Gulf crisis, yet we waged war anyway. She was called repeatedly as part of the parish "prayer chain" to pray for a woman with cancer—who died anyway. I asked, "What did praying for the Middle East do for you and your church friends? Did anything result from your praying for the person with cancer?" She reflected that praying for the Middle East had at least helped some people to locate the Persian Gulf on the map! And praying for the woman with cancer had promoted a good deal of caring toward the family, which was still going on. We were back to the bottom line of prayer for Kierkegaard: *Prayer changes us.*

I amaze myself that I am teaching seminary classes on prayer and leading spiritual retreats because I have often said, "I'm such an agnostic it's a miracle I am a Christian!" For all who share such sentiments, I invite you to begin where Kierkegaard began: *Praying changes the pray-er.* Teresa of Avila could never achieve peace free of conflict. Jesus' own desire for solitude was constantly interrupted. So simply look at *the struggle to pray as a gift* that develops compassion in the heart of the pray-er: "And he had compassion for them" (Mark 6:34).

People say prayer is mainly a matter of coincidences, and I am inclined to agree because the more I pray the more I notice the coincidences increase! People who begin praying soon discover unexplained opportunities for compassion–and celebration.

PRAYER EXERCISE 20: The Gift of the Struggle

I invite you to visualize some area of your life where you are currently struggling. Then picture yourself as if you simply gave up on the struggle. Let this be a way to renew your commitment to the *gift* of the struggle. (Suggested readings: Mark 1:35-38; Colossians 1:29.)

Creativity: The Benefits of Wasting Time

The very idea of "using" prayer for some cost-effective benefits is a contradiction! The danger of speaking about the "benefits" of prayer is that we really need to seek God for God's sake. But that is not the place where many *begin*. People start praying when they have a problem. So others of us need to be convinced of some benefits—if only to find in the end that the "benefits" are deceitful. Like a mirage in the desert, they create a deeper thirst for Godself and draw us to service.

☐ The purpose of *intentional prayer* is to make us *more prayerful* in our active life in community (see theme 3, "The Discipline of Community"). Cultivating our ability to listen for "the still, small voice" has a direct correlation with our ability to be attentive to the voiceless ones of the world, the poor whom Jesus called blessed. Thus the discipline of solitude (theme 4) yearns for its completion through the discipline of service (theme 6). The missing link is the discipline of the heart and mind (theme 5), "formation" of a discerning heart to know how best to serve.

The story of Mary and Martha presents a marvelous picture of contemplative prayer: Mary's wordless listening, sitting at the feet of Jesus (Luke 10:38-42). And as Martha's accusation surely indicates, such "nonsense" seems to be a waste of time, and time is money!

☐ Luke uses the word *squandering* or *wasting* in his story of the Prodigal and the Perfectionist. In the far country, the Prodigal *squandered* his money in reckless living. The Prodigal's gift of ingenuity is obvious by his creative scheme for getting his money ahead of time! But his virtue of *creativity* degenerates into the vice of reckless squandering.

And the older sibling's one obvious gift of *faithfulness* degenerates into the vice of dutiful resentment.

The "father" in the story embodies *both these qualities* of faithfulness *and* creativity in a "redeemed" form. His "redeemed duty" is manifested as *faithfulness*: He waits faithfully for the lost child. And his "redeemed squandering" is manifested as *creativity*: He engages in "redemptive waste," killing the fatted calf in a wild celebration of love (15:22-32)!

In the next story, Luke picks up the theme of "squandering" again in reference to the Dishonest Manager: "Charges were brought . . . that this man was squandering his property" (16:1). After the manager's scheme to win friends by writing off half their debts, "His master commended the dishonest manager because he had acted shrewdly [creatively]; for the children of this age are more shrewd [creative] in dealing with their own generation than are the children of light" (16:8). But immediately Jesus extols faithfulness: "Whoever is faithful in very little is faithful also in much . . . " (16:10-13).

☐ Our third path home, the way of transformation, calls us to imitate the "father," to integrate faithfulness *and* creativity. Luke would have us see Mary as the redeemed Prodigal, who now "creatively squanders" some precious time at the feet of Jesus (10:38-42).

Christian tradition has been aware of Luke's idea: We speak of the "Prodigal" Son, prodigious, ingenious, creative. And Luke's teaching on prayer (11:1-12; 16:10-13) calls for persistence.

Prayer makes us creative *and* keeps us persistent. These two values are conveyed in the dual names for the community of believers in Isaiah 43 (exercise 2): *Thus says the Lord who created you, O Jacob—the conniving one; the One who formed you, O Israel—the struggling one. Fear not, for I have redeemed you; I have called you by name, you are mine.*

The name, our name, *Jacob* means "the conniving one," and its redeemed form calls forth the creativity of the community and its individual members. The name, our name, *Israel* is given after wrestling all night with God at the River Jabbok: "You shall no longer be called Jacob, but Israel, for you have [struggled] with God and with humans and have prevailed" (Genesis 32:28). Wrestling in the night of prayer, we get a new name: Jacob Israel. Live up to your name: Creative Strugglers.

Fear not, for I have redeemed you, Jacob: Your gift of creativity is in your waste. Be prodigal enough to "waste" some time with God! A bit of "redeemed squandering" transforms burnout into creativity! You might decide to throw a party for someone, or even yourself! Take a week for silent retreat. "Wasted" solitude rescues me from taking myself too seriously.

Fear not, for I have redeemed you, Israel: Your gift of faithfulness is in your struggle. You have attempted many times to cultivate an intentional time of daily prayer, only to falter and give up. Jesus' struggle for solitude is your struggle. Simply to stay engaged in the struggle is a gift of faithfulness: "For this *I toil and struggle* with all the energy that [Christ] powerfully inspires within me" (Colossians 1:29, italics added; see Philippians 3:12-17; 1 Timothy 4:10).

I am always cautious to promote the value of solitude for pragmatic reasons. Yet we can love God *with our* minds, holding the benefits of solitude before the mind's eye. British scientists R. A. Brown and R. G. Luckock[1] have provided myriad examples of breakthroughs that have come to well-known scientists as they were daydreaming, dreaming, sleeping, meditating, or in a relaxed state of mind: Kekulé dozing at the fireplace, coming up with the theory of the Benzene ring; Einstein boarding a streetcar in Zurich discovering $E=MC^2$.

☐ Benefits of solitude vary with personality type, but the list includes: perspective, insight, realizing forgiveness, reordering priorities, creativity, peace, rest, release from stress. As one person said, "It makes me nicer to be around," a good invitation to explore solitude!

PRAYER EXERCISE 21: Designing Your Daily Solitude

Individual or group experience: I invite you to take three pages in a journal and list the (1) *barriers* that get in the way of your solitude, (2) *benefits* you have experienced, and (3) *bridges* to solitude—prayer methods that have worked for you or methods you would like to try.

You will get the most value by sharing your responses *one-on-one* with another person.

Group: After the sharing in pairs, the leader may solicit responses from the group; perhaps list the three categories on newsprint.

Methods for Method-ists: Bridges to Solitude

John Wesley, like his brother Charles and their mother Susanna, was remarkable, schooled in the classics of Greek, Latin, and Hebrew, the theology of the Protestant Reformation and Catholic mystics, especially Ignatius of Loyola. Wesley's followers were ridiculed as "methodists" because of their emphasis on "methods" that could assist our own prayerfulness.

Call them methods, disciplines, exercises, or practices of the spiritual life—they are simply like bridges. You do not live on a bridge; it merely provides ready access from one shore to the other. To use another image, spiritual exercises are like pipelines laid in the desert to transport water to thirsty people. What is important is not the conduit but the life-giving water. There is always a danger that spiritual practices may make us "religious" rather than "Christian."

☐ I approach prayer "methods" with some caveats. First, we can easily become spiritual junkies, experts in a hundred "techniques." (A word I will not use because it buys into commercialism and manipulation—"mastering the techniques.") The goal of spiritual practices is to surrender our mastery of things to the Mystery. The great hymn writer Isaac Watts urged us to distinguish *between the skill and the grace of prayer.* "The skill is but the outside, the shape, the carcass of our responsibility. The grace is the soul and spirit that gives it life, vigor, and efficacy, that renders it acceptable to God and of real advantage to ourselves."

☐ A second caveat is attributed to a Roman plebeian: "The same shoe does not fit every foot." Each one is a particular personality type whether analyzed by the Myers-Briggs Type Indicator, the Sufi Enneagram, or by one's best friend.[2] For example, "visualization prayer" may seem impossible for some. Yet I have grown spiritually more by trying exercises that were *not* suggested for my type than I would have by staying only with those that initially felt comfortable.

"Pray as you can and not as you can't," great mystics have said. But unless I try praying some ways I think I can't, I don't know how I can! So the ancient proverb is not an excuse to avoid trying new methods; yet recognize that not all forms of prayer are equally suited to each.

Christ is the way, the journey, not the guides we may meet along the way. In words attributed to Matthew Arnold, "Be committed to Christ, and for all the rest be uncommitted."

☐ Here are some methods to assist our presence with God: *singing hymns* (or reciting the words); using *recorded background music; praying with scripture, lectio divina* (see exercise 28); *daily lectionary readings,* along with some *liturgy* such as the Episcopal daily office; the Presbyterian Church (USA) provides the common lectionary readings in a *Mission Yearbook for Prayer and Study,* so one can also be praying for the world; *praying the Psalms* (exercise 25); *tape recording prayer exercises or scriptures* then playing it back for yourself; *combining prayer* and *physical exercise,* walking, biking, jogging, tai chi, back exercises; *breathing* and *body prayer* (exercises 8, 11, 13, and 38); *intercessory prayer* (see chapter 16 and exercises 31, 32, and 33); *contemplative silence* (exercise 6); *centering prayer*[3] (repeated use of a phrase or a word, exercise 30); *spiritual readings (A Guide to Prayer for Ministers and Other Servants* or *A Guide to Prayer for All God's People*[4] and especially Christian biography;[5] *the prayers of others* (such as John Baillie's *Diary of Private Prayer*); *keeping a spiritual journal* (exercise 26);[6] *paying attention to dreams;*[7] *praying with icons;*[8] *the Jesus Prayer* (exercise 38);[9] *being attentive to nature,* "I lift up my eyes to the hills" (Psalm 121:1).

☐ Finally there is a spiritual discipline Ignatius believed was the one essential prayer form if we were stripped of outward aids: *the daily examen.* Socrates said the unexamined life was not worth living. Calvin and Kierkegaard could not decide whether it was more important to know God or know self, or which came first. I invite you to this simple "self-reflection in the Presence" at the beginning or ending of each day. Then let it become a gentle habit of the heart throughout the day.

PRAYER EXERCISE 22: A Daily Examination of Grace

(1) Invite Christ, the Light of the world, to walk with you over the past twenty-four hours, gently sifting through the events of the *previous* day.

(2) *Give thanks* for some gift of the day.

(3) *Celebrate God's empowering love* at a time or times when you were loved or were loving;

(4) *Celebrate God's undefeated love* at times when you were less than loving, and hear Christ say, "I know that and I love you."

(5) *Ask God for a specific grace for the day ahead* (for example, in light of your "confession" above, you may pray for the grace of patience, or in light of a difficult meeting ahead of you, you might pray for the grace of listening or discernment).

(6) *Finally, hold before the mind's eye what your life would look like if that grace were granted.* Place "a hidden video" at home or work. Then see yourself walking into the board meeting, your workplace, or home—as whole, as God through Christ already sees you.

Your Personal "Darkroom"

The goal of a set-aside devotional time is to train the spiritual eye to "turn to God in all things, in all things to see God." The mystics are united, and my experience agrees, that some quantity of prayer in early morning yields a special quality for the day, even if your longer time must be later. For an extrovert like myself, used to constant action, my daily retreat period consists of four or five component parts, always beginning with body prayer exercises, including some intercessions and the Lord's Prayer; the daily examen; meditating with scripture; then a period of contemplative silence. Other practices come and go, but these

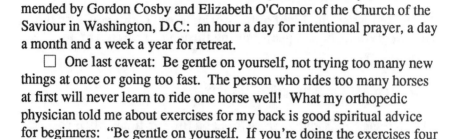

seem essential for me. I know of no better goal than the rhythm recommended by Gordon Cosby and Elizabeth O'Connor of the Church of the Saviour in Washington, D.C.: an hour a day for intentional prayer, a day a month and a week a year for retreat.

☐ One last caveat: Be gentle on yourself, not trying too many new things at once or going too fast. The person who rides too many horses at first will never learn to ride one horse well! What my orthopedic physician told me about exercises for my back is good spiritual advice for beginners: "Be gentle on yourself. If you're doing the exercises four days a week you're going in the right direction; if you drop back to three, you're going in the wrong direction."

☐ In solitude we cultivate roots that support us in crisis. In *Hostage Bound, Hostage Free*, the Rev. Ben Weir tells of his captivity in Beirut, Lebanon.[10] He would recite hymns and psalms (in his head for fear of retaliation); a bare light bulb hanging from the ceiling became for him a symbol of Michelangelo's "hand of God" reaching toward him; the chain that bound him became a kind of "Protestant Rosary" as he said particular prayers with each link; the vertical slats hanging at the window became for him a reminder of the communion of saints, living and dead.

In solitude we enter our spiritual darkroom where we can expose the negatives of the world and of our lives to the Light. There we summon the naked courage to expose our negatives, and when we do we are transformed into positive print—an icon of Christ. The transformation may not be apparent during the specific time of solitude or even in the immediate days, but Kierkegaard was right that prayer is what you do to get your own ground ready.

Theme 5
The Discipline
of the Heart and Mind

CHAPTER XI

Spiritual Re-Formation

The heart has reasons which reason knows nothing about.

—Blaise Pascal, *Pensees*

Everyone who reflects seriously on the spiritual life wrestles with the tension between cognitive learning and mystical experience. We are constantly in danger of losing the creative tension by choosing between mind *or* heart. "The heart has reasons which reason knows nothing about." Contemporary quantum physics affirms this creative tension. That which is real is not *ir*-rational but rather has a paradoxical, *trans-*rational quality, illustrated by the nature of light which mysteriously is *both* particle *and* wave, position and motion—an impossibility! Light illustrates the paradoxical quality of life. Each of us is a particular unique person in a time and space, yet each participates in timeless experiences of all humanity. We desire answers, yet we can hear them only by questioning; we desire to know and be filled, yet can do so only through emptying and unknowing.[1]

Charlie Brown, experimenting with the "new" Crayola crayons, muses to Lucy: "'Teal' or 'cerulean' . . . which color expresses what I'm trying to say here?" He goes on and on, asking which exotic colors would articulate what he wants to say. Finally Lucy interrupts in bold letters: "COLOR THE SKY BLUE AND THE GRASS GREEN!" Now flat on his back, Charlie Brown mumbles, "Get out the black. I'll do a night scene."

Schulz's cartoon is a statement about the spirituality of education. After we take seminars on the most fascinating, new methods for anything—in the field of medicine, sports, business, science, the arts, or spirituality—we often become captivated by the newness. Thinking we

---

have "mastered the techniques," we try out our new skills. At first we are awkward and even a bit cocky. I play the piano for enjoyment, but in the beginning stage of struggling to learn Scott Joplin or Andrew Lloyd Webber's music, I often think of an old proverb: "Almost anyone can play the notes; it takes an artist to create music." The transition often involves some kind of dark night scene, some unknowing, before the light dawns. It is a movement of the heart more than of the mind, more intuitive than cognitive, whatever the field. Spirituality means moving from our "doing" toward what Flannery O'Connor called a "habit of being."

Learning: In-Formation *and* Re-Formation

The movement from exterior skills to interior habit is not so much re-ceiving more *in*-formation as it is experiencing a *re*-formation of the self: The skills are internalized as part of you. You might think back to some simple skill, riding a bike, hitting a baseball, or driving a car. Now it has become an art. It is not as if you no longer think at all; a slight scare while driving can make you instantly attentive and aware of proper driv-ing skills. It can even create a desire for more information, realizing your vulnerability.

The "slight scare" is a helpful metaphor. Often when we are forced into a "cloud of unknowing," to use a title of a spiritual classic we are open to new learning. Conflict is a catalyst for education; it creates the ready seedbed. Robert Coles tells why he uses the "awe-ful" stories of Flannery O'Connor to teach Harvard medical students. Her stories im-pinge severely on the students' sense of self, like radical surgery, leaving them with "a subsequent erosion of that cocksure moralizing inclination [that] sets the stage for a possible gain—the mind a bit cleaner, a bit less self-deluded."[2]

When we refer to some time of difficulty by saying, "It was a good learning experience," we witness the truth of Kierkegaard's statement that suffering is our teacher. Retroactively through prayer an experience of seeming futility may still bear fertile learnings. Prayer is the labora-tory of the spiritual life as research is for science.

Re-Formation and Creativity—the *Kenosis* Pattern

"Imagination is more important than knowledge," Einstein said. A prerequisite for creative imagination and problem solving in any field—parenting, scientific inquiry, international or labor relations—*is to lay aside ingrained assumptions and discern previously unseen possibilities.* I have to become "agnostic" about some of my favorite ideas! It is why Meister Eckhart was so misunderstood when he spoke of the "God beyond God"; he was not rejecting God but our human images of God.

This "laying aside" is the Incarnation: Christ *emptied* himself—*kenosis—the self-emptying* pattern for genuine spiritual formation. This "kenotic" Christ is the model for shaping the mind: "Let the same mind be in you . . . "(Philippians 2:5-11). John's gospel paints it as a picture: The night of the Jesus' arrest, "Jesus . . . rose from supper, laid aside his garments, and girded himself with a towel. Then he poured water into a basin, and began to wash the disciples' feet" (John 13:4-5 RSV). The Incarnation is the pattern woven into the whole fabric of life experiences: Some emptying needs to happen before we can be filled.

While writing this I was "interrupted" by a forestry consultant who stopped by to evaluate a two-hundred-year-old tree shading the study where I write. I thought, *Good—I can learn from him.* So I mentioned that I was using the "tree" as a metaphor of the spiritual life. But overwhelmed by this man's vast knowledge about trees, for a moment I thought I would have to scrap the image entirely; my little knowledge had been a dangerous thing. Suddenly I was bankrupt! But my "agnosticism" concerning the tree carried me to a new level where I could reclaim the image to use in this book. The interruption bore fruit.

Re-Formation: Four Methods in Jesus' Ministry

Unrest and conflict are the birthpangs for our re-creativity. Into this ready seedbed comes Jesus Christ—causing disciple-learners to perceive the truth "from below," out of their own struggling—which is prayer. The Christ of the gospels is the Source and Pattern for uniting affective and cognitive learning.

Four educational methods are integral pigments in the gospel portraits of the Master Teacher: discerning *questions*, coupled with *story-telling and story-listening*; the creative power of *example*; and *creative repetition*, i.e., repeated acts and themes that become bearers of ritual. These four embody a powerful and practical model of integrating mind and heart.

PRAYER EXERCISE 23: Prayerful Reading of a Gospel

I invite you this week to a simple practice of prayerfully reading through *one* of the four gospels, preferably in one sitting (probably the gospel of Mark because it is the shortest, the earliest, and moves quickly). Visualizing the events, make your own inner "Hollywood" video, allowing yourself to participate in or observe the scenes.

CHAPTER XII

Questions and Stories

Be patient toward all that is unsolved in your heart and to try to love the questions themselves like locked rooms and like books that are written in a very foreign tongue.

—Rainer Maria Rilke, *Letters to a Young Poet*

Questions are a primary component of Jesus' teaching. They intrigue us to self-revelation as well as to the mystery of God. What do you want me to do for you? What do you think? Which one, do you think, was a neighbor? Who do the crowds say that the Son of man is? But who do you say that I am? If you love only those who love you, what reward do you have? If you greet only your brothers and sisters, what more are you doing than others? Simon, son of Jonah, do you love me more than these? . . . Do you love me? . . . Do you love me?

Like Locked Rooms: The Lure of Questions

The lure of questions in Jesus' ministry is to call us through *childlike inquisitiveness* to cultivate the qualities of *resiliency and compassionate intelligence*.

☐ Questions are *the seedbed of learning*. Like a catalyst in a chemical reaction, questions speed up the process. They embody "the lure of experience," mathematician-philosopher Alfred North Whitehead's wonderful phrase, drawing you into deeper mystery.

Sometimes, the actions of Jesus or his followers deliberately stir up questions. One sabbath Jesus' disciples walk through a grain field and begin to pluck the grain. The "religious folk" ask, "Look, why are they doing what is not lawful on the sabbath?" Jesus answers one question with another, a lure to their own tradition: "Have you never read what

---

David did, when he was in need and was hungry . . . how he . . . ate the bread of the Presence, which it is not lawful for any but the priests to eat?" (Mark 2:23-28 RSV). Similarly, on another occasion: "What is written in the law? What do you read there?" (Luke 10:26).

Other times, questions are drawn from mundane symbols of necessity: "Show me the coin used for [paying] the tax. . . . Whose likeness and inscription is this?" (Matthew 22:19-20).

☐ *The inquisitiveness of a child* is lifted up as the model of the spiritual life. "Truly I tell you, unless you change and become like children, you will not enter the [commonwealth] of heaven. . . . Whoever welcomes one such child in my name welcomes me" (Matthew 18:1-5). The parables are a catalyst for this childlike learning; they get people buzzing with curiosity; Jesus is asked to explain his riddles (Mark 4:10-13). *Encyclopedia Brown's Record Book of Weird and Wonderful Facts* reports that the average four-year-old asks 437 questions a day!

In Growing Young, Ashley Montagu urges us to cultivate the qualities of a child—while not remaining at an arrested stage of childhood development. "It is—the need to love others and be loved; the qualities of curiosity, inquisitiveness, thirst for knowledge; the need to learn; imagination, creativity, openmindedness, experimental-mindedness; the sense of humor, playfulness, joy, the optimism, honesty, *resilience and compassionate intelligence*—that constitute the spirit of the child."[1]

☐ *Resiliency and compassionate intelligence*: Surely these are two *fruits* of Christian spiritual formation, just as surely as *inquisitiveness* is its seedbed. The way we grow spiritually mature is paradoxicAlly by cultivating childlike—though not childish—characteristics.

PRAYER EXERCISE 24: Hospitality with a Child

As a kataphatic, physical way of praying, "follow Jesus" by physically enacting his invitation to *welcome a child* (Matthew 18). Think of a child, one of your own, a niece or nephew, a grandchild, a godchild, a neighbor's child, or one in the church nursery. Find a way to spend some time with this child, playfully and prayerfully, but also expecting that *you are the one who will learn from the child.* Notice childhood characteristics, questions, stories, behaviors, barriers, and any of your own discomforts. In a journal, record your observations. Spend some time reflecting on the experience in a group or with another individual.

If we view the person we are with as our "teacher," a relationship becomes mutual; genuine service is not just "doing a good deed." (You might also try this with an older person or a disabled child or adult.)

Compassionate Questions: A Way of Loving Neighbor

Our purpose is not to become good questioners but good listeners. If we barrage a person with *probing* questions, even the tone of voice can be annoying. Questions that come from the heart reflect an *interest* in the other's well being: *Inter-esse* means our "common being."

Jesus' creative method of inquiry combines education *and* compassion: "As he went ashore, he saw a great crowd; and he had *compassion for them,* because they were like sheep without a shepherd; *and he began to teach them,*" inquiring and instructing (Mark 6:34-35, italics added).

Montagu's "compassionate intelligence" illustrates this combination of *teaching with compassion.* "They were all amazed, and they kept on asking one another, 'What is this? A new teaching—with authority! He commands even unclean spirits'" (Mark 1:27). What astounds folks is that Jesus' teaching *includes compassion* for hurting people. The "new teaching" is *the wedding of education and compassion.*

"Compassionate education" is a *two-way process of discerning ourselves and the needs of others,* so that when we reach out our hands in service we will not miss the mark. I once heard about an outdoor church bulletin board which read, "Christ is the answer!" and a graffiti artist had scribbled, "But what's the question?" Jesus communicated *even the truth of his messianic identity* by means of questions: "Who do people say that I am? . . . But who do you say that I am?" (Mark 8:27, 29). Every community organizer or marketing firm knows the value of questions to establish the need for which you may then offer appropriate service.

The same is true in ordinary human relationships. When my children one by one reached their teen years, they began to deal with how to relate to people in new and threatening situations. I gave them my own heard-learned wisdom: If you feel at a loss for words in a classroom or a social situation, ask a question! Thoughtful questions show an interest in another; they create dialogue. "Win the right to be heard" runs a motto of the Young Life organization. Before giving answers, questions establish a relationship of trust and become a bridge to loving our neighbor.

Through interested questions and attentiveness to people's responses we begin to feel something of what they feel. *Compassion* is a visceral, physical word, as Andrew Purves has shown. In Hebrew *compassion* is derived from *raham* the word for *womb*: By sharing our pain, God births us to new life! In the New Testament *compassion* is *splagchna*, the Greek referring to the "wrenching of the bowels" in solidarity with another's suffering. The King James translators used the guttural phrase "bowels of mercies" (Philippians 2:1). The word is used as a verb *only by Jesus or about Jesus* to refer either to himself or God.[2] *Teaching with compassion* cannot be merely intellectual, "off the top of my head," but embodies Christ's struggling in my soul in solidarity with others' suffering.

The people who interrupt us often seem "like sheep without a shepherd," unaware of their real needs. Only in the process of "compassionate intelligence," through questions that leave us open to others and God by "unlearning" our own prescribed answers will our programs for hunger, redevelopment, education, or counseling be of real service to others. Unless like Mary we listen to the teaching of Christ in our neighbor, then like Martha our service may lack compassion and miss the needs of the very people we want to serve.

Compassionate questions pave the way for service, but they must first come from being in touch with our own pain. If they don't, they will only distance us from our neighbors' pain.

Honest Praying: Soul-Searching Questions in the Psalms

When Jesus said, "Go and do likewise," at the end of the Parable of the Good Samaritan, he knew this would be impossible for the lawyer unless he became *like a Samaritan himself*, in touch with some rejection in his own life. Our best efforts to do good often painfully confront us with our own inner questionings of the soul. At the time we never welcome it. "Personally I am always ready to learn, although I do not always like being taught," Churchill once said. Being "Christian" can make us more sensitive and our struggle more difficult.

Clumsily, painfully, we pray our way deeper into the Mystery of divine suffering love through our foiled and failed attempts to show compassion: The world breaks everyone . . . *The Good News is that we can choose to view these inner questionings as a positive movement.* In *Letters to a Young Poet*, Rainer Maria Rilke offers a Christian perspective.

> I want to beg you . . . to be patient toward all that is unsolved in your heart and to try to love the *questions* themselves like locked rooms and like books that are written in a very foreign tongue. Do not now seek the answers, which cannot be given you because you would not be able to live them. And the point is, to live everything. *Live* the questions now. Perhaps you will then gradually, without noticing it, live along some distant day into the answer.[3]

We go through many nights of the soul wrestling with God: Why is there such suffering? Even and especially when we try to do good? How can we create justice with love? This is the stuff the Psalms are made of.

In the Psalter *disturbing questions* are invited right into the struggles of praying, becoming *soul-searching prayer*. One's own "self-talk" along with taunting questions of others become one's prayers: "Why are you cast down, O my soul, / and why are you disquieted within me? / . . . I say to God, my Rock, / 'Why have you forgotten me?'. . . / my adversaries taunt me / . . . 'Where is your God?' " (Psalm 42:5, 9-10).

Rabbi Harold Kushner would not have wrestled so deeply with the question *When Bad Things Happen to Good People* except through the suffering of his own son's disease. Unless we face squarely our own doubts of the soul, our attempts to figure out others' problems and teach life's lessons will be merely a projection of our own unresolved struggles.

PRAYER EXERCISE 25: Praying A Difficult Psalm

Try praying one of the "negative" psalms, for example Psalm 22, "My God, my God why . . .?"—on behalf of someone whose suffering is so intense that he or she no longer may believe in God. Pray it as if Christ on the cross is praying it in you for that person. Or pray a psalm of praise as intercession dedicated to someone with cognitive or speech impairment. Or try writing a psalm that would express the feelings of a person with disabilities or the feelings of oppressed people.

Daytime Talk, Nighttime Talk—and Story

But people are spiritually hungry for more than just unsettling questions —or simplistic answers. My own education rightly emphasized the dangers of easy answers because then people avoid their own pain and have no ownership in the process, receiving premature or even dangerous solutions. Yet I found people yearning for something more than self-insight. Struggling with this impasse, I rediscovered something obvious in the format of the gospels.

Story provides a simple yet profound method *to integrate mind and heart.* Storyteller Robert Bela Wilhelm describes the three kinds of languages: One is *our daytime talk,* our directive language that has its source in the left brain: Take out the garbage; analyze this problem; it's time to eat; find a solution. It is the language of intellect, analysis, productivity. *Nighttime talk* has its source in the right brain. It is the language of lovers and poets, of musicians, novelists, and artists; it is the language of intuition, imagination, and creativity and can even be a rich source for solving "daytime" problems!

What links these two is a *third language—storytelling—*a combination of the daytime and nighttime talk, bridging and integrating both.

Storytelling is daytime talk because it makes sense. It is also nighttime talk because, like a dream, it is rich in images that can happen in a story but not in real life.[4] Stories create inner space where we can hear the echoes of the Presence. They act as a shuttle to weave our conscious and unconscious selves together.

Questions and stories work together as primary tools of learning, like the brush and the paint to the artist, like the musical score and the instrument to the musician. Questions give birth to stories; stories spawn new questions. "When your children ask you in time to come, 'What is the meaning of the decrees . . . that the Lord our God has commanded you?' then you shall say to your children, 'We were Pharaoh's slaves in Egypt, but the Lord brought us out . . .' " (Deuteronomy 6:20-25). A question about doctrine is not answered with logical information, but by re-telling the story. In the gospels Jesus sometimes tells parables to respond to a question, other times to stir up more questions.

The Gospel story within *the believing community integrates both languages,* the daytime language of creeds and codes, the nighttime language of poetry and hymns, conveyed via the third language of story. There is scientific research showing the unitive effect of story. Whereas technical material stimulated the left sphere of the brain, and music and art stimulated the right, stories actually stimulated both spheres.[5]

The Hebrew understanding of *heart* includes both cognitive and imaginative dimensions: "Trust in the Lord with all your heart [both intuition and intellect], / and do not rely [solely] on your own insight [understanding, intellect]" (Proverbs 3:5). "So teach us to count our days that we may gain a *wise heart*" (Psalm 90:12, italics added).

Christ's Story-Journey—and Journaling

The story format of the gospels and scripture as a whole is meant to transform believers to face the toils and the conflicts and the sufferings that the community has faced, personified in its Messiah's suffering and overcoming. Our story-journey becomes part of the larger story.

We need constant reminders of the value of storytelling in teaching and preaching, and narrative theology. But I am concentrating on stories for spiritual formation in personal, interpersonal, and family contexts.

☐ *Reading spiritual biographies* or short stories about another's journey (such as *Guideposts*) has a transformative, mentoring effect through the power of example.[6] By recalling the presence of Christ in the lives of other "saints," we participate in "the imitation of Christ."

☐ *Keeping a spiritual journal* can help us to listen to our own internal story-journey. Writing journal reflections on experiences of an individual day integrates that single *jour* (day) with our lifelong *journey*. Dag Hammarskjold's *Markings*, Henri Nouwen's *The Genesee Diary*, and Reinhold Niebuhr's *Leaves from the Notebook of a Tamed Cynic* are classic.

PRAYER EXERCISE 26: Keeping a Spiritual Journal

A diary records what happened: "Went to supermarket. Saw Bob." A journal records your response to it: "Went to the supermarket. Saw Bob, who just lost his job. I reflected on my own career changes; it drew me to pray for him." Try journaling in response to: (1) scripture, (2) conversations, (3) dreams, (4) meaningful quotes, (5) life experiences.[7]

Stories in Counseling, Spiritual Direction, and Families

On the interpersonal level, *stories can be helpful in one-on-one counseling and spiritual friendship and in families.* A good spiritual friend or counselor will use questions to help a person look more deeply into oneself. Yet when people really want and even need answers, "there are so many stories more beautiful than answers," as Mary Oliver put it.[8] So when a person presents an impasse, and you keep thinking of a story from your own experience, or another's experience or from a book or film, it is good to pay attention. Telling it (disguising the names, of course) may create a real connection to the need at hand. Meaningful story creates a "mini-trance," a pregnant pause, where the self is momentarily suspended, opened to Mystery, to the Presence, to Creativity.[9]

Resiliency: The Quality of Redemptive Stories

Redemptive stories have a paradoxical twist, *often containing an element of terror that generates resiliency.* The most powerful stories, ones that transform us, whether parables of Jesus or stories from novels or movies or life, have within them some paradox and mystery, often comic elements that reverse our normal way of seeing, and tragic elements that engender visceral feelings of compassion. *Resiliency* is a secular word that conveys the spiritual quality of resurrection at work.

In my work as a chaplain, brain-injured people and their families have often been my teachers, the source of my learning about the brain. Here is truly the paschal mystery: nearly all creative research on the brain is born out of the devastating suffering of many. In one such book, I found the following story about storytelling."[10]

☐ During the holocaust, a small group of people survived a death camp. A researcher asked the leader what they had done differently to survive. It seems this little group would gather and prolong their sparse meals, sometimes for hours, conversing and picturing the people they would hope to see again—eating roasts and potatoes, cakes, and wine.

The bottom line of this research is that *the brain can provide nurture from sources other than food.* What we believe about ourselves can allow us to conquer pain and even survive; it may well change our susceptibility to illness. Jesus was right: "I have food to eat that you do not know about. . . . My food is to do the will of [the One] who sent me and to complete [that] work" (John 4:32-34). Storytelling nurtures the discipline of vocation, our "why" to live as well as our "work" for a living.

☐ In a hospital chaplain training program, a new student chaplain was assigned to visit Marie Smith, a patient with terminal cancer who had requested a visit. This seminarian's first real encounter with death, he was overwhelmed with the stench of necrotic flesh as he went down the hall. As he entered the room and saw her ashen color, he thought he would throw up, but then remembered from somewhere that it helps to sit down and put your head in your hands. He sat that way for four or five minutes, and the sickness did lessen. But when he looked at the woman, instantly he felt so embarrassed that he just got up and left the room. Feeling that he had failed, he went to the meditation room to sort things out. He decided he would tell his supervisor the next day that he was resigning from the program, and maybe even from seminary. But the next morning before he got the chance, the supervisor found him. Marie had just called again. *Oh no,* he thought. "Well, this time she just wanted to say thanks. After she called yesterday, she wished she hadn't; she was so sick she didn't feel like talking and surely didn't want any minister preaching to her. She said, 'The chaplain who came must have sensed that. He just sat down, bowed his head, and prayed for me for maybe five minutes. And then he gave me the most loving glance and left. Of all my times at this hospital, this is the most meaningful visit I ever received.'"

Once when I told this story, someone asked, "But the chaplain wasn't really praying, was he?" His intense identity with her pain *was his praying, his yearning for her,* the biblical "bowels of mercies," *splagchna,* visceral prayer.

This is what the Reformation was meant to be all about, not merely *in*-formation about God but continuing character *re*-formation, individual and communal. It was not to discover God in Godself, *but God in relation to lived human experience, and nothing does this as well as stories of faith.* Christian education ought to be renamed "spiritual formation"; it is "the education of desire," transforming the affections of our hearts. And the most powerful vehicle is a story that embodies *the example of a lived life.*

CHAPTER XIII

Creative Example

My life is my message.

—Mahatma Gandhi

Christ was in the world incognito *and that was His* kenosis.

—Nicholas Berdyaev, *The Divine and the Human*

Discipleship is a primary term for spirituality, especially in Reformed, evangelical, and Wesleyan traditions, shaping disciples according to the pattern of the Master Teacher, yet in a creative way so that each becomes a unique self.

The Patterning Process: The Imitation of Christ

Disciples are called to be like children—imitators, malleable, inquisitive. The Master Teacher invites us to learn about prayer by praying: "One day, Jesus was praying in a certain place. When he finished, one of his disciples said, 'Lord, teach us to pray, as John taught his disciples.' He said to them, 'When you pray, say, Father [Abba] . . . '" (Luke 11:1-2). From this we learn several things about ascetic theology, the theology of spiritual experience.

 • *Example creates a thirst in others.* Observing Jesus' genuine life of lived-out prayer creates a desire in others to pray.

 • Only from the vantage point of *children* (Greek *paides*) can we pray the model prayer, addressing God as Parent. We speak of "pedagogical" methods, and its root *paideia* is "discipline" or "training" (Hebrews 12:8; 2 Timothy 3:16); it conveys Calvin's essential spiritual quality—*being teachable.*

 • The words *teach us to pray* communicate a pattern of loving God with mind and heart: *teach us*—the left-brain dimension; *to pray*—the right-brain dimension. We need to integrate systematic theology with

---

ascetic theology, teaching about God with lived experience of the Presence.

● *The way to learn to pray is by praying.* "Lord, teach us to pray," is answered by, "When you pray, say. . . . " The pattern of the Lord's Prayer tells us how to pray: Learn to yearn by yearning. This is the value of a spiritual retreat and the reason for including *prayer exercises* in this book. Yet even our retreats get filled with words about God instead of actual time praying. No one can *teach* us to pray except by inviting us to experience our own inmost yearnings. That is what Schweitzer meant when he concluded, "[Christ] will reveal himself in the toils, the conflicts, the sufferings which they shall pass through in his fellowship, and, as an ineffable mystery, *they will learn in their own experience who he is.*"[1]

Guarantors of Our Identity: The Lived Life

"I want to preach the Gospel with my life," Charles de Foucauld often said. Young adults and "recovering adult children" of all ages want what Erik Erikson called "guarantors of our identity." It has often been said that the Christian faith is "more caught than taught," and this kind of mentoring needs to be recognized as the one form of "Christian education" that should have priority. In training sessions for church teachers I have often said, "You are the curriculum!" It is what Gandhi meant when he said, "My life is my message."

The power of example is classically expressed as *The Imitation of Christ,* writings attributed to Thomas a Kempis.[2] There are only three ways to teach, Schweitzer said: by example, by example, and by example.

☐ The gospel portraits lure the reader into the patterning process of Messiah's painful birth, ministry of love and conflict, death and resiliency. For a beginner, just to read the gospel of Mark in one sitting can be a life-altering experience as witnessed by the long-playing, one-person stage-reading of *The Gospel of Mark* by off-Broadway actor Alec McCowen (see exercise 23). Through the pattern of the suffering-rising Messiah, the gospels lure us from being admirers to being "followers" of the Way.

Discipleship by imitation is the Great Invitation: "Come to me. . . .

Take my yoke upon you, *and learn from me*; for I am gentle and humble in heart" (Matthew 11:28-29, italics added). It is the Great Commission: "As the Father has sent me, so I send you" (John 20:21). "Go therefore, and make disciples of all nations, baptizing them . . . and teaching them to obey [listen to] everything that I have commanded you" (Matthew 28:19-20). Servant-leaders are born via imitation: "So if I, your Lord and Teacher, have washed your feet, you also ought to wash one another's feet. For I have set you an example" (John 13:14).

☐ The powerful irony of the gospel stories is that the Master-Teacher is constantly emptying his own cultural and intellectual knowledge and *becoming like a child*. "Not my will but yours be done." In the story of the persistent Canaanite woman (Matthew 15:21-28), Jesus at first ref-uses to heal her daughter. It is not in his job description: "I was sent only to the lost sheep of the house of Israel" (v. 24). Immediately, how-ever, Jesus' habit of emptying himself took over. *Is that true, Abba? That is why you sent me, isn't it?* Question. Listen. Be empty. But she persists, "Even the dogs under the table eat the children's crumbs." Jesus empties his cultural prejudice, his "logical knowledge" of who is worthy, and heals her daughter. Jesus turned inward; the habit of practicing emptiness won out.[3]

● Jesus is the model for using foiled and failed attempts to love our neighbor to drive us deeper into our spiritual struggle: "Now my soul is troubled. And what should I say—[Abba], save me from this hour? No, it is for this reason that I have come" (John 12:27). On the cross Christ cries out in utter abandonment: "My God, my God, why have you for-saken me?" (Psalm 22:1). Compassionate teaching finally means solidarity with our deepest questioning of the soul: Jesus' life has become the message.

● The Christ-life is also the pattern for understanding and redeem-ing all of life's experiences: Some emptying needs to happen before we can be filled. *Kenosis* is the model for genuine spiritual "formation," the creative transformation of suffering. "For to this you have been called, because Christ also suffered for you, leaving you an example, so that you should follow in his steps" (1 Peter 2:20-21; see 3 John 11). "Be imitators of me, as I am of Christ" (1 Corinthians 11:1; see Philippians 3:17). What minister today would have the audacity of the apostle Paul to say that?

Imitation of Christ: A New Look

The imitation of Christ has traditionally meant "ethical" imitation. The call that I am extending is to an underlying "spiritual" imitation, to practice the habit of continual self-emptying (Philippians 2:1-11). Only a spiritual imitation can be the source of genuine ethical character development.

New issues of medical science never before dreamed of, along with the high rate of technological change, have caused increasing relativity of ethical guidelines in our time. More than ever we need discernment in a highly situational society, not an external, ethical copying, but *imitation* as an indispensable *inner spiritual model for discernment.*

This constant turning to God for guidance in the moment requires grace as the Source of our ethical life. In Reformation theology ethical actions have always been viewed as a response to an inner work of grace. It is not imitation that brings about our relationship with God, but our relationship that makes imitation possible.[4]

☐ One reason for much of the negative reaction against the classical view of the "imitation of Christ" has been precisely because it centered on the ethical question, "What would Jesus *do*?"—the theme of Charles Sheldon's classic *In His Steps.* Despite the admirable example of "following in Jesus' steps," it seemed to be something *believers must do,* rather than something *God does in us.* Many choices Jesus made were conditioned by his time and place. No one now would be helped by a literal imitation of Jesus' walking down the middle of first-century Roman roads while teaching! What would Jesus do in the twenty-first century? The imitation of Christ is not a series of single acts but a habit of being: What would Jesus *be doing? Being* one with God is manifested in Jesus' *doing* good.

The one thing Jesus would always be doing is *praying, yearning for one thing, to do the will of the One who sent him.* That is what I mean by spiritual imitation of Christ. This kind of "imitating" creates the movement (illustrated in the *kenosis* diagram—**image 4**—on page 89) from willfulness to willingness, from mastery and control of my life toward Mystery and surrender, from independence to interdependence, from a calculative to a contemplative life, from a quest for security to a quest for discovery: What is life (God) inviting me to?

Nicholas Berdyaev refers to a remarkable passage where
Kierkegaard relates Christ's *kenosis* to our call to imitate Christ: "The
call to those who labour and are heavy laden comes from the humiliated
Christ, not from Christ in glory. But the Christian Church does not wish
to recognize the kenotic Christ. . . . Christ was in the world *incognito* and
that was His *kenosis*."

Berdyaev encouraged Christians to enter into and experience the
struggles and trials of doubters, even atheists, and not look down on
them: But it is with difficulty that men and women "bear the *incognito* of the Divine and the *kenosis* of Christ": We prefer the Christ of
majesty.[5]

☐ And so another reason for negative reaction to the traditional
"imitation of Christ" is the impression that one must always set a *good*
example. People who try too hard to be good become immune to grace.
I am advocating being a *genuine* example, to expose our need for grace.

The *kenosis* model means *imitating Christ's vulnerability*: "Now
my soul is troubled." It is a movement from trying to be a *good example*
to trusting you can be a *genuine example*. This is not an excuse to flaunt
our sins, but to pay attention to failure as well as faith in the examples of
Rahab and David and Ruth and Mary Magdalene and Peter, to pay attention to Paul's foolish boasting as well as his struggles.

● *Parents* can be better examples to children by admitting their
vulnerability, not pretending they are faultless, but sharing personal
struggles and how God helped them through some unlikely personal
conflict or circumstance. By admitting our weakness, we develop
children's strengths and creativity: "This problem has me stumped too.
How can *we* solve it?" To enlist the assistance of the person we are
trying to help is the imitation of Christ in community: "*We* must work
the works of [the One] who sent me while it is day; night is coming"
(John 9:4, italics added). Genuine parental authority, like that of the One
for others, is established "from below." Christ emptied himself.

● *Lay persons* who teach youth and adults can set a genuine example by sharing a problem, and how prayer or a text of scripture or an
unexpected encounter with a friend helped in dealing with it. Vulnerable
faith is the essential warp for the woof of printed curriculum. Christ
emptied himself.

● *Pastors* can minister to laypeople more effectively by modeling this vulnerable kind of faith, modeling that we too stand before the cross in need, "one beggar showing another beggar. . . . " By asking others to pray for us, by asking for their opinions, by exposing our naked need for grace, we bear a witness "from below." Our most effective witness, our most powerful stories are born of times when we have been the recipient of surprising grace. Prayer is when we are re-converted. Christ emptied himself.

The first funeral I conducted after being ordained was for an out-of-state, nonagenarian, inactive member. I was so judgmental: These people who move away and don't care enough to join another local church! And her family couldn't even meet me till just before the service. It was then I learned this woman and her husband had served in China as career mission workers for the Presbyterian Church, and our congregation was "home" in the USA all those years! I was emptied, humbled by a discomfiting bit of grace; I died a bit and rose again that morning; Christ was formed in me a little more that day, my attitude and theology of funerals forever changed.

We receive little inspiration from the description of an *ideal* example: We could never be like that. But there is great power in the *genuine* example of one who has confronted problems with faith and resiliency. It is the deeper *imitatio Christi* to empty oneself continually of cultural prejudice, to become vulnerable, to listen for God in each moment. What Jesus would be doing is obeying the *shema—listening*. This is the *kenosis* paradigm.

Pastiche: Finding Your Unique Style

Positive imitation is what J. R. R. Tolkein meant when he spoke of the idea of *pastiche*, a French word referring to *repetitive imitation of one great artist by a pupil*—writer, musician, painter, athlete, sculptor—until the pupil hones a genuine style of his or her own. You are apprentices of the Master: Keep practicing *pastiche*, keep making copies until the Christ is uniquely and genuinely re-produced in you.

But if we cannot make this spiritual re-formation happen, what can we do at least to foster it? I am proposing that spiritual formation occurs when *a repeated rhythm of worship* (corporate as well as private) *and service* become the intentional "curriculum" for Christian discipleship.

The gospels convey the idea of example in picturesque language using theological *narrative*; the letters of Paul convey the same idea using theological *concepts*: "Let the same mind be in you that was in Christ Jesus, who . . . emptied himself. . . . Therefore God has highly exalted him" (Philippians 2). Yet these words were not written as abstract theology: They form an early Christian hymn *sung from the heart, over and over*, creative repetition through ritual. This is the pattern of incarnation, the self-emptying *kenosis* of the Servant-Messiah taking shape in the minds *and* hearts of believers.

PRAYER EXERCISE 27: Recalling Spiritual Mentors

Who were some "spiritual mentors" for you, genuine examples of faith tested in real life? As you name them, give thanks. You may also include writers (I include C. S. Lewis). Tell someone else how these people influenced you, inviting those you tell to the same experience.

CHAPTER XIV

Creative Repetition

It was discovered that Ice Age paintings in a cave in southern France were made up of layer after layer of pigment. The evidence was that they had been drawn and redrawn, and so were perhaps an early record of the human spirit expressing its sense of an eternal rhythm through reenactment and ritual.

—Ernest Boyer, Jr., *Finding God at Home*

The process of the imitation of Christ is enacted in the community's story through repeated acts of corporate worship, praying with scripture, and being with "the least of these."

Habits of the Heart: Being Formed and Re-formed

Blaise Pascal and Simone Weil, living in France three hundred years apart, one Catholic, the other Jewish, were both brilliant "outsiders" in a lover's quarrel with the church. Each could pray, "Lord, I believe; help my unbelief." Despite serious doubts, each experienced a mystical conversion to Christ. Yet each recognized the value of repeated ritual for its long-term effect in forming the Christian person and re-presenting Christ to the world.

☐ *Through repeated acts in the liturgy of the community, Christ is re-presented*, verbally and nonverbally. If you want to write, read other good writers; if you want to be good at music, listen to good music; if you want to be a good athlete, attend athletic events. Over time, repeated ritual acts, e.g., table grace at home, sermons from the pulpit and the questions or frustration they evoke, listening to scripture, experiencing baptisms, and breaking bread in communion, stir our childlike curiosity to ask, "What is the meaning of these signs?"

☐ *Creative ritual* is the seedbed for spirituality. When children ask, "What is the meaning . . .?" tell the story (Deuteronomy 6:20-25)! When liturgy creates curiosity, love the questions like locked rooms, like books in a foreign language! During the years of greatest religious repression in the former Soviet Union, many methods were tried to discourage people from attending church, from outright persecution to benign neglect. Yet many grandmothers carried babies to church in their arms. Authorities who had outlawed printed "curriculum" figured, What harm could a bit of religion do to a few old women and children? But the repeated scriptures of the liturgy and the power of maternal example produced a new generation of Christians and a spiritual hunger in former Soviet countries!

In ancient caves of France, Cro-Magnon humans mixed pigments, drawing and redrawing paintings on cave walls, appreciating the miracle of nature's rebirth all the more with each repetition.[1] This is very close to Kierkegaard's meaning of repetition: The real self and the ideal self become congruent by means of the redemptive power of Christ the Pattern. One of Kierkegaard's prayers is good liturgy and good Christian education:

> O Lord Jesus Christ . . .
> Thou art both the Pattern and the Redeemer,
> and again both the Redeemer and the Pattern,
> so that when the striver sinks under the Pattern,
> then the Redeemer raises [us] up again,
> but at the same instant Thou art the Pattern,
> to keep [us] continually striving.[2]

By constant exposure to the Pattern, the ideal becomes attractive to us, until we recognize the reality of our emptiness, which creates the readiness for the Redeemer, for grace. By means of creative repetition in ritual, one's real self becomes more congruent with the ideal self.

☐ *Our spiritual journey of faith is like a spiral staircase.* We come around again and again to the same issues of doubt and faith, but always at a deeper level. "Lord I believe; help my unbelief."

Creative repetition is *not* redundancy. Much of our spiritual formation in Christ, including these words, is simply relearning what we already know only at a deeper level. People will say critically they had gone to such and such a church all their lives but never heard the Gospel. Now I am convinced that many of us only "hear" the Gospel when some brokenness occurs in our life. Then we re-discover what we already know. It is a shift from knowing with the mind to knowing with the heart.

I used to complain that a lot of church people wasted time "reinventing the wheel," in arriving at personal faith or in arriving at a committee decision. I am much less judgmental now. Insight is not transferable. I recognize in my own life that I must feel an "ownership" in the ideas of others from the bottom up before they become my own. The incarnation helps me to see that patience with "repetition" in meeting after meeting of a church committee can be as spiritual as repeating the liturgy! When you find yourself repeatedly annoyed over a conflict, it may not be just the issue or the person: It may be God wrestling with you, as God wrestled with Jacob.

☐ "Evangelical" Dietrich Bonhoeffer and "Catholic" Thomas Merton point out that *the Psalms were meant to be sung or said in rhythmic repetitiveness in community and in solitude.* Calvin said the Psalms contain an "anatomy of the soul," a mirror of all its emotions. So repeating the Psalms is one of the ways the soul is kept clean before God, expressing its anguish and anger, joy, and confidence. The Psalms were Jesus' prayerbook, so praying them is a primary way of patterning Christ: The Servant-Messiah still prays the Psalms in us. All our affections— sexual, spiritual, emotional, and physical—are "baptized" and offered to God. The Psalms affirm that when you were baptized into Christ's death, every part of you was baptized; your anger as well as your ecstasy can be continually surrendered as birthpangs of resurrection. Madeleine L'Engle writes in *Out of Egypt* that she prays five psalms a day, the entire Psalter each month.

☐ *The four gospel stories are also meant to be read again and again.* The repeated cycle of the Christian year reminds us that the risen Messiah continues to join us in our human journey from beginning to end. Through dark times we await the advent of some something new, but the joy of the Messiah's birth is silhouetted by an anxious and questionable parental relationship; a childhood trauma as a foreign refugee; an adoptive father who becomes an absent father; a series of wilderness temptations; a delayed career, at age thirty entering an itinerant ministry filled with three years of conflict; a lifelong premonition of a violent death; a betrayal by a loyal friend. "The world breaks everyone," including Jesus. But by experiencing our humanity—the violence of the cross, the emptiness of the tomb—the life of the suffering-resilient One becomes *the prototype of strength out of weakness:* the continuing work of the Spirit, an ongoing Pentecost!

Praying with Scripture—the "Second Inspiration"

The Christian community also imitates Christ as it prays the scriptures. Through praying with scripture, *the Word becomes flesh* in us again and again. As a child and for most of my life, I had the impression that one's personal devotional life consisted of reading the Bible, then saying your prayers–two distinct actions. I am only beginning to learn what it means that "all scripture is inspired by God," *God-breathed* (Greek *theopneustos,* 2 Timothy 3:16). Meditative reading of scripture is the "second inspiration" as the Spirit breathes the ancient Word into our flesh.

In the fifth century, Benedict of Nursia, who can rightfully be claimed by all Christians because he lived before any major church splits, gave us a method as old as the psalm-writers: the *lectio divina,* the "divine" or "prayerful" reading of scriptures. It is a simple method: Read a short text prayerfully, *over and over, like a cow chewing her cud,* until you are led to "delight" in God," a phrase repeated often in the Psalms. Meditating on Psalm 119:9-16, Theophan the Recluse commented, "To pray is to descend with the mind into the heart, and there to stand before the face of the Lord, ever-present, all seeing, within you."

PRAYER EXERCISE 28: Praying with Scripture

The twelfth-century Carthusian monk Guigo II divided Benedict's *Lectio* into a fourfold experience, beginning with silence: *reading* and rereading the text; *meditating*—looking at the text in its contexts (see pages 55 and 56); then *praying* over a short section of scripture

until it leads to *contemplating*—"Lost in wonder, love, and praise,"
in Charles Wesley's words. Contemplation is what the psalmist
means by "Take delight in the Lord, / and [God] will give you the
desires of your heart" (37:4). It is Luke's image of Mary sitting at
the feet of Jesus. Then the Word becomes flesh in us through spirituality embodied in service.

Three particular ways of "praying" the text have for centuries
been of great assistance in forming the heart and mind. Begin with
silence.

● *Visualize a narrative scene in scripture.* Set the stage: Is your
village back-then? Or contemporary? Create your own Hollywood
"inner video"—*sense the smells, sounds, touch, taste.* Many spiritual
writers—Ignatius, Francis, and Teresa of Avila, who had a great
deal of trouble quieting her soul, found that inner visualization had a
powerful character forming effect. Calvin recognized the value of
visualization just as "coloring books" help children experience the
Word.

● *Dialogue with the participants,* inwardly, or by writing in a
journal, concluding by conversing with Jesus in the gospel episodes.

● *Repeat a particular fruit of the text*—usually a phrase or word
—over and over, in rhythm to the breathing. Often a parable of
Jesus' is punctuated with a pithy, memorizable question or saying.
The centurion says to Jesus, "Only speak the word, and [your] servant will be healed" (Matthew 8:8). The Good Samaritan story ends
with both a question, "Which ... do you think, was a neighbor to the
man who fell into the hands of the robbers?" and a pithy quote: "Go
and do likewise" (Luke 10:36-37). The repeated phrase acts as a
"centering prayer," leading to emptied contemplation. It helps to
recall one to prayer during the day.

An Inner Library—Scripture Memory

Western society is fascinated with novelty (yet I notice that young folks
will see the same movies many times!), viewing repetitive acts as boring.
That accounts in some ways for the decline in scripture memorization,

for centuries important in evangelical spirituality. And in Eastern Orthodox churches, a high percentage of the liturgy consists of repeated scriptures. It is a continuation of the Hebrew tradition of phylacteries, key verses of the Torah inscribed on the doorposts or on tiny parchments worn close to the heart and treasured in the mind. This is one primary way for the faith to endure in repressive societies that forbid printed materials.

In my chaplaincy work, I have had a rare privilege of being with a vanishing generation of Americans who, if I suggest it during worship, can repeat favorite scripture verses. Some can say even long portions such as the Beatitudes "by heart." When eyesight has failed some of them, an "inner spiritual library" of scriptures, hymns, and prayers is a great source of comfort and courage.

Prisoners and pilots, hostages and newscasters, mothers under stress, and patients undergoing health crises witness to the value of this inner library of spiritual treasures, planted in the heart in years of abundance, harvested in years of desert thirst.

PRAYER EXERCISE 29: Building Your Own Inner Library

Reclaiming scripture memorization can be a good means of practicing the Presence. Call up your "internal card catalog" and list in your journal verses that have nurtured you. As you take a shower, do chores, or ride to work, a verse of scripture may come to mind and be repeated over and over throughout the day, acting as a centering prayer. Tell someone the "history" of the meaning a verse has for you or, in a group setting, recount favorite scriptures to each other.

The Teaching: The Messiah in "the Least of These"

Jesus' teaching in the Sermon on the Mount has long been recognized as the catechism (*didache*) to instruct new Christians. "Blessed are you poor" (Luke) or "poor in spirit" (Matthew). And this is the *didache*—the

---

teaching that only as we are in touch with our own poverty of spirit can we imitate Jesus' teaching by example.

Christian spirituality is cultivating that "sixth sense" of attentiveness. "Keep awake therefore, for you do not know on what day your Lord is coming" (Matthew 24:42). But the surprise in Matthew's next chapter (25:31-46) is that "Divine Royalty" is camouflaged in "the least of these" *right now*—in the hungry, the thirsty, the homeless, the naked, the sick, and the prisoners. By contrast, "religious" folk are inattentive, assuming that the hungry and the sick are poor folk and nothing more. Elizabeth Barrett Browning speaks to this attentiveness:

Earth's crammed with heaven,
and every common bush aflame with God.
Only those who see take off their shoes,
the rest sit round and pluck blackberries.

When we stand on holy ground, we see with new eyes that lure us to attend to the Servant-Messiah in the faces of the least of these, which is the discipline of service.

Theme 6
The Discipline of Service

CHAPTER XV

Service as Prayer

Jesus still comes to us in the distressing disguise of the poor.

—Mother Teresa of Calcutta

What do you do after you say, "I believe"? You become like Christ, but that is not something you do at all. It is something that happens in you as you pray, following the *kenosis* pattern of Christ's constant self-emptying. And the one authentic fruit of this inner imitation of Christ is loving service: "I am among you as one who serves" (Luke 22:27). Jesus' verbal parables are re-presented today through stories, including music, art, and drama (see theme 5, "The Discipline of the Heart and Mind"). We will now explore how Jesus' nonverbal, parabolic actions are re-presented through our ministries of service, and how liturgy integrates both *verbal* and *nonverbal actions,* becoming "the service *of* worship" (theme 6).

Mime and Imitation: Silence in Jesus' Life and Ministry

The gospel portraits of the Messiah present the balanced pattern needed for the spiritual life of the believer: community and solitude, teaching and service, and vocation, i.e., constant discernment of one's purpose on this earth: "Not my will but yours be done" (Luke 22:42). Silence is to service as being is to doing: If our action does not arise out of contemplation, it will miss the mark, damaging ourselves and those we try to serve.

Secrecy in the gospel portraits embodies the Messiah's self-presentation to the world. This indirect communication is not just a political

---

---

tactic to avoid being crucified too soon: It is the messianic secret. Jesus frequently charges individuals not to tell others about his acts of healing, and he chooses to reveal his messianic identity indirectly, "Who do people say that I am?" . . . "But who do you say that I am?" (Mark 8:27, 29). As Screwtape says to the young apprentice devil regarding "'the Enemy,'" "He cannot ravage. He can only woo."[1] Any spirituality that ravages, suspect it as more anti-Christ than Christ.

And even though the gospels portray Jesus approving the titles "Messiah" and "Son of God," these are on the disciples' lips, not his own, and their content is a suffering-serving *Child of Humanity* ("Son of Man," Mark 8:31-33). Jesus' favorite self-designation is this puzzling "Child of Humanity" that functioned like the parables to invite curiosity, serving as an intentional disguise. It could refer to a wide range of possibilities, from a humble individual (like Ezekiel), to a divine messianic Deliverer, to the suffering faithful saints, to generic humanity.[2]

This ambiguous title, Child of Humanity, is uniquely on Jesus' lips in the gospels and bears witness to divine communication via indirection and silence. Jesus' silence, especially at his trial before Pontius Pilate, is a powerful theme in the Japanese author Shusaku Endo's best-selling *A Life of Jesus*. This Messiah puts flesh on Karl Barth's statement: "It is a terrible thing when God keeps silence, and by keeping silence, speaks."[3] Unlike the religious leaders who "do all their deeds to be seen by others" (Matthew 23:5), Jesus' life is his message: Jesus "being there for others" *is* the experience of the Transcendent, as Bonhoeffer put it. Jesus is "the One for thers," the Prototype of divine love on earth.[4]

The word *mime* comes from the Greek *mimesis* (imitation). The ancient mimes were not completely silent as they acted out life situations and mythical dramas. So the Servant-Lord authenticates his words by wordless action. Christ genuinely embodies "the imitation of *God*"— a theme in Hebrew scriptures and preserved in Paul: "Be imitators *(mimetai)* of God . . . and live in love, as Christ loved us and gave himself up for us" (Ephesians 5:1). The more we participate "in Christ," the more we begin to "mimic" that authentic spirituality of the One for others who "came not to be served, but to serve, and give his life" (Mark 10:45). We represent the Messiah whose loving action grew out of silence.

Silence in the Life of the Believers

The silence in the life of Jesus has a correlation in the life of the believers. "Whenever you give alms, do not sound a trumpet before you. . . . Whenever you pray, go into your room and shut the door and pray to your Father. . . . When you fast, put oil on your head and wash your face, so that your fasting may be seen not by others but by your Father who is in secret" (Matthew 6:2, 6, 17-18). The roots of the tree do their work in the underground of secrecy; yet their work is indispensable to the beauty and productivity of the visible tree. The quiet work of prayer is inseparable from the work of genuine service, and *both* are the continuing work of Christ in us.

One classic meaning of *mimesis* is "re-presentation." The Christian community continues to re-present the Mime, making the Messiah real in the world. "The church is the church only when it exists for others. . . . The church must share in the secular problems of ordinary human life, not dominating, but helping and serving. . . . It is not abstract argument, but example that gives its word emphasis and power," wrote Bonhoeffer.[5]

But this call to wordless witness does not mean that we never speak about the inner life of prayer. That was the flaw of the lost piety at the time of my own seminary education. The gospels are full of Jesus' teaching on spiritual disciplines, obvious in the words above from the Sermon on the Mount. But Jesus' teaching on prayer comes directly out of his own life of service and is directed to the inner circle of believers. To those outside, the message is presented indirectly via parables and parabolic acts of service.

The hidden, underground work of prayer is meant to be manifested in visible works of compassion: "You are the light of the world. A city built on a hill cannot be hid. No one lighting a lamp puts it under a bushel basket. . . . let your light shine before others, so that they may *see your good works* and give glory to your Father in heaven" (Matthew 5:14, 16).

Silence: Another Dimension—the Messiah *Incognito*

Contemplative prayer involves a clear vision into the reality of human suffering, not an escape from it. Imitating Christ means becoming aware of the transcendent Presence in "the least of these." Gandhi invites us to "recall the face of the poorest and most helpless [person] whom you have seen, and ask yourself if the step you contemplate is going to be of any use to [that person]. . . . Will it restore [that person] to control over [his or her] own life and destiny?"[6] This is genuine imitation. It should be no surprise that Gandhi, while remaining a Hindu, died with a picture of Jesus at his bedside.

So the secrecy theme has a third dimension: The risen Christ is concealed in the unlikely folks to whom we think we are going to show the light! The tricky part is that our light is only reflected light, always from its Source: "I am the light of the world." "You are the light of the world" (John 8:12; Matthew 5:14).

The Source is paradoxical: Light breaks through the very folks we are called to serve, igniting the light in us who serve. It is the Emmanuel model: The risen Messiah is the eternal Presence, revealed as a stranger, a guest. Jesus still rises to meet us in the poor, in the crucified of the earth. Unless we recognize this, we will miss the camouflaged Messiah: "Just as you did not do it to one of the least of these, you did not do it to me" (Matthew 25:45).

The idea of the Messiah concealed in the faces of the afflicted is not unique to Jesus; it has a long history in Jewish tradition. Like a priceless Rembrandt sketch that predates a painting, this tradition of the hidden Messiah is now revealed in full color in the gospel portraits of Jesus. The Hebrew *anawim* include all the poor and marginalized: the sojourners, the oppressed, the lame, the hungry, the thirsty, the sick, the rejected, the grieving, the suffering, the afflicted, the wretched of the earth.

It is what contemporary talmudic scholar Emmanuel Levinas is saying in *Difficult Freedom*. "The respect for the stranger and the sanctification of the name of the Eternal are strangely equivalent. . . . To feed the world is a spiritual activity."[7] The lives of the *anawim* require our service, not because they deserve extra pity, but because of whom they signify. Through them God can speak to us most clearly!

Both our inward seeing *and* outward doing is prayer. "Even though your works are lowly, and unimportant in themselves, perform them solely for God and with as much care as if you were binding up the wounds of Christ," wrote Henry Suso.[8] To have our eyes opened to the surprising Mystery, the secret Paradox, is what spirituality is all about.

Ministry Burnout: Prelude to Spiritual Purgation

Even though Christ has made us God's own, in our spurts of spiritual growth, redeemed prodigals may become perfectionists, and redeemed perfectionists may become more prodigal. We may oscillate between the two spiritual paths.

At some points we try deepening prayer and intentional spirituality, and Christ is in our desert sharing all our temptations that go along with the inner spiritual life (Matthew 4): We can get addicted to our spiritual highs! At other points, especially if one had a strict upbringing, we may embrace the world's good and sensual gifts, and Christ is there too: "The Child of Humanity has come eating and drinking" (Luke 7:34).

Yet there is a fine line between enjoying and becoming attached to either. As William Blake wrote,

[One] who binds to [oneself] a joy
Does the winged life destroy;
But [one] who kisses the joy as it flies
Lives in eternity's sunrise.

Either path can get us into trouble again unless it frees us from attachment and leads to the third path of transformation.

The religious path of denial may be marked by spurts of sincere prayer but may leave us bankrupt again, naively pious and irrelevant. The worldly path of affirmation may be marked by ethical intensity and prophetic service as we attempt to "take on the world's problems," but may leave us—with Martha and Elijah—cynical, superior, and burned out from too much serving (Luke 10; 1 Kings 19). Is it possible for such "ministry burnout" to become a "spiritual purgation" of our attachments, a creative dis-illusioning, re-forming the Christ within?

We desperately need the third spiritual path, like that of Mary, one that integrates the paradox of the prayer *and* action, where ministry burnout can become the prelude to renewed service.

Mary and Martha:
"Being with" Prerequisite to "Doing For"

These few powerful verses (Luke 10:38-42) form the skeleton for understanding contemplative prayer and life in the anonymous spiritual classic *The Cloud of Unknowing*.

Genuine service is not a way of just *doing* the Gospel but a way of *being* the Gospel, transforming us from "doing for" to "being with" the *anawim*. When Friedrich von Hugel became a spiritual director for Evelyn Underhill, one of the first questions he asked was how much time she spent with "the least of these." Her decision to take time weekly with the poor revolutionized her life, grounding her spirituality in compassion. (If you have not tried exercise 24, I invite you to do so now.)

☐ Mary's contemplative "listening at the feet of Jesus" has rendered a timeless prophetic service to all humanity! "To clasp the hands in prayer is the beginning of an uprising against the disorder of the world," wrote Karl Barth.[9] Mary's prophetic service baptized the intellectual and spiritual powers of women *and* men as being just as sacred as manual labor. By integrating being with doing, her praying became a rich union of *both contemplation and manifestation.*

Mary had the prophetic audacity to break the cultural tradition that dictated that the primary services women could offer were physical—food, lodging, or sex. In the gospel saga Martha and Mary (and Lazarus?) frequently extended their gift of hospitality in Bethany to this homeless Galilean: "The Child of Humanity has nowhere to lay his head" (Luke 9:58). But in this instance, Mary recognized that the timely form of hospitality Jesus most needed was that of listening and appreciation.

Mary chose the better *portion*: "I have food to eat that you do not know about" (John 4:32). Hers was the better *helping*: "The first service that one owes to the fellowship consists in listening to them," wrote Bonhoeffer.[10]

THE DISCIPLINE OF SERVICE

Mary quietly made the audacious claim that nurturing the spirit, for Jesus and herself and perhaps for other disciples present, was more important to the ultimate revolution of values than feeding the body; she, as a woman, made the radical claim that "being" is the indispensable prerequisite for authentic "doing" for both men *and* women. Mary's *example* of claiming space to learn and listen *was* her service. And she attentively discerned the felt need of their guest for spiritual companionship, for someone to appreciate the Word *(logos), because what he was saying expressed who he was.*

☐ We now look at Mary's sister: Martha's beautiful gift was hospitality: "A woman named Martha welcomed him into her home" (Luke 10:38). But she was addicted to her gift and therefore distracted from her guest by "too much *diakonia,*" too much good ministry. She has all the marks of codependent behavior: *blaming* others instead of *claiming* space and help from them.

Without the taproot of contemplation our serving degenerates into anxious manipulation. Jesus said to Martha, "Mary has chosen the [better] portion" (10:42 RSV). "Portion" *(merida)* is a food word, as when we invite a dinner guest to take another "helping" or "serving." Mary had chosen *the better serving.*

Attempting to take care of everyone's needs *by herself and in her own way* (alone, *monè*), Martha dished up anxiety instead! Mary, by her attentive listening, discerned the better "serving," the more appropriate "helping." It was better not because prayer is better than service, but because *Mary's way of serving united the two, prayer of contemplation and prayer of manifestation.* "To each is given the manifestation of the Spirit for the common good" (1 Corinthians 12:7). There is no split here between prayer and action. Inward attentiveness is manifested as outward attentiveness to her guest: *Both are prayer.*

☐ Redeemed prodigals and redeemed perfectionists both need the path of transformation to keep the two sisters of service and prayer together in peace. Through the discipline of service, falling in love with the world's afflicted and falling in love with Jesus form a mystical union: "Just as you did it to one of the least of these . . . you did it to me" (Matthew 25:40).

On a human level, it would seem that Mary was wasting valuable

resources—in John's version, costly perfume too! (John 12)—while
Martha went ahead with the practical, no-nonsense work. Time is money:
We are programmed to fill every moment with productivity. But what
are we producing *for*?

Join Mary in "wasting time with God"[11] so that your doing can be
centered, as clay must be centered at the still point on the wheel in order
to be at the potter's service. Failure in contemplation leads to crisis:
Without being attentive to our attitude in serving and the purpose for the
things we produce, even good things may enslave the ones who do them
as well as those who have the good done unto them.

Contemplation prepares the poor, earthen clay of my life to manifest
a thing of beauty. In a recent journal entry,the vase occurred to me as a
symbol of emptying oneself before God to be a receptacle for beauty and
compassion with others:

The Vase

I pray for
the grace
to sit at
the feet
of each
person I meet
and see Christ
in their face.

Ascetic listening with God provides training (Greek *askesis*) in attentive listening for the suffering-rising Christ in others. And if we fail
to listen, we will miss the needs of those we try to help.

The great symbol of the faith for John Calvin was *the heart aflame
with devotion to God and the hand outstretched in service to neighbor*.
This is the same genuine piety represented by the Michelangelo's *Pieta*,
Mary tenderly caressing the lifeless yet life-giving body of Jesus. It is
truly an icon of integrative piety: loving Jesus with the heart by touching
and embracing the Christ in human suffering.

Mary's quiet prophetic service baptizes our *being with* as the indispensable prerequisite of authentic *doing for*.

PRAYER EXERCISE 30: Praying with Mary and Martha

I invite you now to pray with scripture using the familiar story of
Mary and Martha (Luke 10:38-42). Read it. Pay attention to its
context, sandwiched between the story of the Good Samaritan's
service and the Lord's Prayer and teaching on prayer. Use the form
of exercise 28, "Praying with Scripture."

● Visualize the scene, as you walk toward the house, a favorite
place of respite for you; being welcomed by Martha; then being in
the house.

● Converse with the two key characters, Mary, then Martha.
Looking at each woman's face, let her tell you how she feels. Experience smells, colors.

● Let yourself become "Martha" as you now pray to Jesus:
"Lord, don't you care that everybody has left me to do this work by
myself?"

● Then picture Jesus speaking to you by name: "_____, you
are anxious and troubled about many things." Spend several minutes telling the Lord about "the many things" in your life now that
concern you.

● Hear Jesus speaking to you again by name: "_____ only one
thing is necessary," over and over. "One thing is necessary."

● If you could condense all the sermons you've heard into just a
single word (or short phrase), what is the one thing necessary for
your life right now? Allow a word to rise within you. Don't censor
it; then continue to repeat it slowly, over and over, in rhythm to your
breathing. You might visualize it like the "Pac Man" image, absorb-
ing each distraction. Or think of your "word" as a little conveyor
belt, carrying each concern, one by one, into the heart of God.

● Spend at least *ten minutes* repeating your word again and
again, becoming "Mary" now, quietly sitting at the feet of Jesus.

This is "centering prayer." I encourage you to use this method
of praying over at least two to three months, using your "word" to
see if this kind of praying helps to "center" you on your active
journey.

CHAPTER XVI

Samaritan Stewardship: Direct and Indirect

Though it finds no name for [the Divine], whenever the afflicted are loved for themselves alone, it is God who is present. God is not present even if we invoke [God], where the afflicted are merely regarded as an occasion for doing good.

—Simone Weil, *Waiting for God*

Mary represents a "redeemed prodigal"—serving by "use-less" prayer—now freed to "squander" some time and resources at home with God instead of away in the far country. The "good" Samaritan represents a "redeemed Martha"—the wounded healer—praying by "use-ful" service in the world. The Samaritan's twofold ministry of direct and indirect service is the model for balanced Christian stewardship.

Samaritan Service—By Presence *and* Absence

The *redeemed* Samaritan freely chose to serve directly, pouring oil and wine as his own inner wounds connected him to the wounds of another. But as a *redeemed* "Martha," he also freely chose *not to do all the serving by himself.* He paid the innkeeper to do the balance of the caring on his behalf. Paying attention to the ratio of direct and indirect service has far-reaching consequences *at all levels of the spiritual life, physical, financial, emotional, and intellectual.*

The Samaritan's indirect service highlights *a ministry of absence* by creative withdrawal.[1] The Samaritan was physically present to the wounded man, pouring on oil and wine and transporting him to the equivalent of a hospital. Half of his stewardship was direct. But his caring continued by paying the innkeeper, the nursing home, the psychiatrist, the hospital, the rehabilitation center. He continued his ministry *in absentia.* The other half of his stewardship was praying by paying.

There needs to be a balance of direct and indirect care for those close to us, as well as for people around the globe. My Jesuit friends have helped me see that the risen Jesus joins us in these missed opportunities, interruptions, and conflicts. To know that the lving Christ is present with us is to be freed from geographical limits.

TheMessiah sets the pattern: "It is to your advantage that I go away" (John 16:7). Sometimes we care best for our loved ones by leaving them in the care of others. In times of too much success when people wanted to acclaim Jesus as *the* prophet and make him king, "he withdrew again to the mountain by himself" (John 6:15). Jesus was interrupted on his way to an important pastoral call to Jairus—young, dynamic leader of the synagogue—whose daughter was ill. A chronically ill woman touched his robe. Jesus stopped. The disciples were irritated, then word came: "Do not trouble the master any longer; the little girl is dead" (Mark 5:21-36). But Jesus paid no attention; he went to Jairus' house anyway and brought resurrection for the child. In the story of Lazarus' death in John 11, Martha and then Mary explode to Jesus, "Lord, if you had been here, my brother would not have died" (vv. 21, 32), and the crowd (v. 37) expressed the same anger.

You can become the lightning rod of others' anger: *If you had been here. . . .* Every caregiver professional or family member knows the sick feeling of arriving just minutes too late in a crisis. We identify with the line in *Jesus Christ, Superstar*: "There's too little of me!"

When you are caught needing to be in two crises at once, you often get a gnawing feeling for the person you cannot be with. By releasing each yearning thought repeatedly with each exhaled breath—while driving, while walking down a hospital corridor—by praying, you participate in the resurrection existence of Christ, *transcending barriers of time and space.*

PRAYER EXERCISE 31: Kything Prayer

Kythe in Scottish means "to feel close to," "to visualize another as though present," as we say, they are kith and kin.[2] Center your

thoughts and picture yourself in the Light; picture the person you
want to pray for in the Light. Hold the face in your mind's eye; then
picture yourself with that person; you might place your arms and
hands in an X shape across your chest as you "hold [her or him] in
your heart" (Philippians 1:7). After a few minutes, exhale, dropping
your hands, releasing your loved one to the arms of God, letting go—
the hardest job we parents or caregivers have!

PRAYER EXERCISE 32: Dedicating Menial Chores as Prayer

As you mow the lawn, take out the garbage, clean the toilets, or
make the beds, dedicate these times "with special intention" for migrant workers or chambermaids, for any who must earn a living via
menial labor. Everything becomes prayer, if you mean it so.

Intercession: Loving by Proxy

Intercessory contemplative prayer becomes a means of loving people
from a distance, *in absentia*. It is what people mean when they say, "It's
good just knowing you are there."

☐ *Service becomes prayer.* We intercede "by proxy" through our
voting, writing our representatives or being the representative, supporting
agencies like Bread for the World that advocate for the world's hungry,
or the Sierra Club and Cousteau Society that advocate for the environment in places we cannot be.

In organized walks for hungry and hurting people we intercede with
our feet: We walk because they walk. When Rabbi Abraham Heschel
marched with Martin Luther King, Jr., at Selma, he was quoted as saying: "I prayed with my legs as I walked." Heschel's academic title at
Jewish Theological Seminary, professor of ethics and mysticism, illustrates the union of action and prayer.[3]

One of the indirect ways many serve is by volunteering time and
expertise on the boards of charitable institutions. But we still need some
quotient of direct service with the *anawim*, and board members who

spend time "being with" the people they serve are immensely more valuable than those who serve at arm's length.

John was serving on an ecumenical housing board and reported with enthusiasm to his church's council about the first start-up unit. When asked where the project was to be built, on which side of certain demographic markers, he had to admit he did not know where the street was. Perhaps if this board, which was under fire for not having enough minority representation, had spent some quotient of time being with the poor, "praying" by walking around, "wasting" time with the poor (God), meeting on their turf, the new project might better target the people's real needs.

Service at arm's length from the ones we serve (witness many government programs) will often miss the mark. Martha and Mary stand as a prophetic summons to our society which puts the emphasis on the "doing for." Unless we restore the neglected portion of "being with," our service (Greek *diakonia)* may enslave ourselves and the very ones we are trying to serve. Because the Samaritan poured on oil and wine directly and transported the wounded man himself, he was not asking the innkeeper to do anything he himself had not already done. Authentic service by proxy needs to be grounded in some hands-on deaconing.

☐ *Prayer becomes service.* We simply cannot be everywhere or give to every cause or do every act personally. e are easily "distracted by many things when only one thing is needful." So in struggling to be free of many things and discern the important thing, we often procrastinate.

But I am learning with Ignatius "to pray in all things," even in my limitations and procrastinations. I think about volunteering at Habitat for Humanity on a Saturday, but I put it off for weeks. I look at envelopes from charitable agencies piling up on my desk. I glance at the daily to-do lists, people to call, write. I have the normal human feelings of frustration.

But with some releasing litany—often for me it is a shortened version of the Jesus Prayer, "Lord Jesus Christ, have mercy"—you can inwardly offer these procrastinations as they come to mind, one by one. Let each breath serve as a positive arrow of compassion, instead of a negative feeling of guilt! Through many such prayings you are receiving discernment. You will have prayed for the urgent tasks that absolutely demanded to be done along the way, and you will be prompted to some action regarding the remainder: volunteer a bit of time; make a phone call; write a check—or throw away the envelope with one more prayer! With only a slight "tilt of the sail," procrastination becomes *prayerful postponement*, creating a positive bond with many persons and causes! Turn to God in all things, even your procrastinations!

In such ways intercessory prayer becomes a means of "being with" instead of merely "doing for" the others in need. It is loving people *in absentia*. Forbes Robinson, a Cambridge don at the end of the last century, linked prayer and action: "To influence, you must love. To love, you must pray."

It seems foolish to allow compassionate musings about other people to circulate through our minds, to release them to God, and then actually believe that activity makes any significant difference in crises of the world! Yet Gandhi could say: "I am telling you my own experience and that of my colleagues: we could go for days on end without food; we could not live a single minute without prayer." Or as he said another time, "Given the type of life I am leading, if I ceased to pray I should go mad!"[4]

☐ *Intercessory prayer itself is service.* "Being with" others by proxy on a sustained basis will make a difference in how we greet them or speak to them in the next phone call, in how we vote at the next board meeting. For the skeptical part of you, at least you can start with Kierkegaard's idea that prayer changes the pray-er! *Share the sufferer's pain; we must be in this place as one village!*

Intercessory prayer is returning to the *Shema*, listening to the pain of the many in the presence of the One. "History belongs to the intercessors, who believe a new world into being," writes Walter Wink.[5] Intercessory prayer is advocacy, spending time sitting at the feet of the Crucified who is present in the faces of the least. It is *ob*-edience, listening from below.

PRAYER EXERCISES 33: Committee Meetings as Intercession

Here are *group* prayer exercises for your committee or board meetings that help with "being with" those you serve. By the choice of the space where you meet, you can be more attentive to the task as well as the persons you serve (see also Exercise 10: From Committee to Community):

- Lay ministry committee ("Stephen ministers" or deacons) might schedule a regular committee in a meeting room of a local nursing home (perhaps one where you have a member), hospital, or rehab center: Some might sit in wheel chairs or geriatric chairs during the meeting to "walk in another's moccasins." Allow silent prayer time, becoming aware of sounds, smells, sights; then converse about your observations.

- Worship committee: Occasionally, try meeting in the sanctuary, the place where worship actually takes place, spending time in quiet prayer being attentive to symbols of worship. Example: If you are debating the frequency of communion, sit in the chancel around the communion table on which are placed a chalice and plate; prayerfully meditate and pray *before* and *during* your discussion of the issues and agenda.

- Christian education committee: Meet in various church school rooms, church library, etc. Example: If debating an issue concerning pre-school children, choose the nursery and sit in the child-size chairs (if you are able); open with a scripture and silent meditation inviting you to "become as a child." Converse about your experiences and insights.

- Outreach committee: Hold a normal meeting at the site of a local mission project that you fund: Prayerfully and quietly be attentive to bulletin boards, posters on the wall, sights, and sounds.

Stewardship: Giving Back—Directly and Indirectly

Giving back is a powerful metaphor for stewardship in our time, easily understood by rich and poor, committed Christians and those on the way. It gets rid of the elitism of a bygone era expressed as *noblesse oblige*— literally "the obligation of the blessed"—with its connotations of benevolence as a duty and of "nobility" as reaching downward to the masses: "Giving without receiving is always a downward gesture."

Giving back speaks of grace; it is our *debt of gratitude.* Robert Bridges once asked Gerard Manley Hopkins how Bridges might possibly learn to believe. Bridges expected a theological answer. Hopkins said simply, "Give alms." Writing a check may be the first link in an ever more intimate chain of grace connecting us to the Messiah in "the least of these."

Both direct and indirect serving involve ecstasy, *ek-stasis,* "going out from one's status" in life. In acts of altruism the brain releases positive endorphins, akin to peak experiences of beauty and even sexual orgasm. I have always liked the lightness of Karl Menninger's quip: "Money-giving is a very good criterion, in a way, of a person's mental health. Generous people are rarely mentally ill!"

Leaving your *stasis,* in the moment of writing the check for a benevolent cause, or going "outside" your local turf to serve, you experience a kind of "going outside yourself," a momentary cloud of unknowing. The check can be a prayer just as much as physically "being with" a malnourished child. One act is pouring on oil and wine, the other is paying the innkeeper. In either moment, you trust an irretrievable part of yourself to the Unknown. No experience affects the lives of youth and adults as dramatically as direct cross-cultural living, where those with few material possessions become our spiritual teachers: mission in reverse.

The story of the "widow's mite" is often linked in the lectionary readings with the story of Elijah and the poor widow (Luke 21:1, see Mark 12:41; 1 Kings 17:9). The natural attitude, then as now, would be to view widows as objects of charity; "men" with resources should give to "women" have-nots. But in each case, the Bible reverses the cultural assumption, and the have-not woman becomes the giver—the teacher and the hero of the story! "Truly I tell you, this poor widow has put in more than all those who are contributing to the treasury. . . . Out of her poverty [she] has put in everything she had, all she had to live on" (Mark 12:43-44). For Beth at age seventeen, a trip to Africa was transformative; receiving spiritual treasures from the hands of the poor in Malawi created a gnawing sense of the poverty of American wealth.

We do not need to go overseas to meet the "widow" or "Samaritan" who could teach us. A lonely student from India "translated" a Dutch professor's "theologicalese," enabling an overwhelmed first-year woman seminarian to understand. But this bit of "mission in reverse" would never have happened without one lonely, caring glance encountering another lonely, caring glance. Their friendship has continued thirty years. Go overseas, but also glance to see the widow or Samaritan at your elbow.

The Mystical Christ in Human Guise: Two Stories

Direct service with the least of these can mediate the mystical presence of the risen Christ. The spiritual emptying of a cross-cultural experience may begin with a person who at first repels us.

☐ In *Our Old Home*, Nathaniel Hawthorne tells of a "fastidious British gentleman" who visited a Liverpool workhouse, and there saw a child so sickly and wretched that he could not tell what sex it was. This "foundling" followed the gentleman in a mute appeal to be held. "So I watched the struggle in his mind . . . and am seriously of the opinion that he did a heroic act and effected more than he dreamed of toward his final salvation when he took the loathsome child and caressed it as tenderly as if he had been its father."

But Hawthorne neglected to add that *he* was this gentleman! After his death, this was found in his journals: "It was as if God had promised the child this favor on my behalf, and that I must needs fulfill the contract. . . . It was a foundling, and out of all human kind it chose me to be its father! . . . I should never have forgiven myself if I had repelled its advances."[6]

☐ For Simone Weil, the incarnation means that God mediates Godself indirectly: through nature, through attempts to love neighbor, and through religious ritual. The following story integrates all three of these.

A dozen years earlier Lois had experienced "the Presence" (see chapter 4), yet she could never figure out where Jesus "fit in." Working in her garden one summer, she made a recommitment: "This time, I decided that by Christmas I would have the meaning figured out. My image of Jesus probably had not changed much since childhood—that of a person very limited by time and space. Books that discussed the nature of humanity and God, sin, salvation, and so forth, were confusing, sometimes irrelevant, and invariably ended up saying our understanding of Jesus was mainly a matter of faith. It was discouraging."

During this time Lois read *A Life of Jesus* by Shusaku Endo, appreciating his simple, direct repeated thought: that Jesus came to demonstrate the existence of *the God of love* and make it possible for people to know *the love of God*.[7] Equally important, Endo's repeated distinction between a "fact" and a "truth" in the Bible freed her from the dilemma of what she "needed" to believe about Jesus.[8]

That autumn worship took on renewed meaning. She found herself responding, uncomfortably, to the sacrament of communion with emotion. "By Christmas, my target date, I decided I was simply not going to be able to 'figure Jesus out,' and stopped trying. I put the issue aside."

In that same period, through the pastoral prayers in worship, Lois had become aware of a young couple whose fifteen-month-old daughter had a malignant brain tumor; only the wife was a church member, and inactive. In early January, simply fulfilling a duty to distribute the church flowers, she chose their home. Her one simple offer to stay with the daughter resulted in a series of visits to this child every single day over the next month until her death in February.

At one point neither the father nor the mother found themselves able to visit in the hospital. Lois must tell this part:

One Saturday I was alone, holding Lisa in a rocking chair. I had been there about forty-five minutes when I began to wonder just why I was there. Here was a child I had never known healthy. She was comatose by then. I didn't know this family very well. I had no obligation to be there or any reason to believe that my presence was doing anyone any good. In addition it was midmorning and visiting hours did not begin until 1 p.m.! I felt very uncomfortable. Lisa's body stiffened. It seemed as though she knew what I was thinking and was saying, "Don't go." It startled me. I whispered to her that I would stay. She relaxed. About thirty minutes later I felt it was time for me to leave. I never again felt awkward being there or questioned whether I should visit. On Ash Wednesday, shortly after her mother and I left from visiting together, Lisa died.

"I discovered that in the process of putting aside my active search for answers and getting involved with this family, I no longer questioned where Jesus 'fit in'. I had apparently been able to say okay to Jesus, who was no longer limited by time or space. I discovered that I had, in fact, known Christ all along."   During that time of involvement, Lois happened to be reading a small book, *The Silence of God*, by Helmut Thielicke:

> We now see how far-reaching are the quiet words of Jesus. Can you not answer the question of who am I? Are you immersing yourself in the dogmas of my divine humanity, Virgin Birth and the like? *Instead, do something in my name and for my sake as though I were already in your life.* Try to order your life by me. Give a cup of water to the thirsty in my name. Forgive another because I have forgiven you. Surrender to me something to which you cling. Dare to lay bare your soul . . . before me. . . . Be sure that you will then suddenly think differently of me, and find a very different attitude to me, than you could ever suspect or imagine when you sought me theoretically.[9]

Here is genuine *imitatio Christi*. Here is a summons to *mimesis*, the wordless Christ in "the least of these."

CHAPTER XVII

The "Service" of Worship: Silence, Hospitality, Simplicity

Thus we clutch a momentary intimacy in worship when we become momentarily a part of a larger whole, a fleeting strength which we pit against all the darkness and dread of other times.

—Howard Thurman, *The Inward Journey*

Thurman's words speak directly to our "high-tech, high-touch" culture where people are craving both individuality and intimacy. Yet the average church "service" allows few silences for individual reflection and little space for vulnerability to express our joys and hurts.

Our ultimate *service* is to offer the brokenness of the world and of our own lives to the transforming God. Nothing visually manifests this Mystery as powerfully as the Lord's Supper where the signs of brokenness become the signs of blessing. The risen Servant Lord still waits on table: "I am among you as one who serves" (Luke 22:27). "Come and have breakfast" (John 21:12).

The early church's pattern of meeting "on the first day of the week . . . to break bread" (Acts 20:7) is a summons for worship to become service, and service to become prayer. By celebrating the Lord's Supper weekly, the service of worship "serves" to unite prayer *and* action in three specific ways: Communion enriches the inward dimension—*meditation;* it dramatizes the outward dimension—*hospitality,* beckoning us to extend Jesus' ministry of table fellowship with outcasts; and it invites us to *unity and simplicity of life.*

Silences in "the Service": Communion in the Spirit

In celebrating communion, worship becomes more meditative, balanced between pulpit and table: the Word proclaimed and the Word made

---

visual. Both Luther and Calvin advocated weekly communion—still the unbroken practice at Saint Giles' [Presbyterian] Church in Edinburgh, Scotland, ever since Calvin's disciple John Knox served as its pastor.

● *Theologically*, the eucharist proclaims the Incarnation: The invisible Word becomes visible, the spiritual mediated through the material, "God with us" in the ordinary elements of our life.

● *Practically*, all personality types need some blend of *repetitive, kataphatic experience* and *apophatic silence*. Communion enhances both: It is sensual yet primarily wordless communication. From childhood I recall a difference in atmosphere on communion Sundays: The "sermon" was given from the table and titled "communion meditation"; there were more silences in the service. Without silence in worship we fall in love with our words instead of the Word, a particular danger for us of the Reformation tradition.

Frequent communion can also foster shorter, more focused preaching. In a sound-byte culture we should heed Woodrow Wilson's insight that if he had taken more time to prepare a speech he could have said it in fewer words!

☐ There *is* a crisis in contemplation in the church. I began this book with a story of a minister and church member who sadly no longer experienced meaning in worship. Hungry, broken people in the pew will benefit from our *programs* only if they have experienced the *Presence*. Yet ministers often say to me at retreats, "I'm here because I can't worship when I lead worship!" Such an attitude is a contradiction, something like an artist who does not appreciate art: It would surprise the average worshipper and seem absurd to any Eastern Orthodox priest. How can I give a "call to worship" inviting others into the Presence if I am not in the Presence? Of course even with communion it *is* possible to race through "the service" in any church, liturgical or nonliturgical. But because the eucharist creates a more meditative atmosphere, it is more likely that the worship leaders will worship—not merely lead worship. As a practical method of change, many churches have added an early service with communion weekly (initially without hymns, or singing one verse or a chant *a capella*, and eventually increasing the frequency of communion at the later service(s)). Multiple services also foster church growth.

Yet even if you do not promote more frequent celebration of communion, you can begin by creating a "communion in the Spirit," rich silences that the Quakers observe without any outward sacrament!

☐ *Incorporate some intentional silences to leaven the liturgy.* Here is the place to start if you are a pastor or lay leader: Begin by owning your own need. If you find it difficult to worship while you lead the "service," then you are being distracted like Martha by too much *diakonia*! So begin with yourself, and encourage your minister or worship committee to do the same. What would help *you* to center on the Presence of God? Whether you are in the pulpit *or* in the pew, try pausing for a moment of inward prayer, taking a deep breath—perhaps using *Lord Jesus Christ, have mercy*—and exhale: after the anthem, before standing (or sitting) for the next response; before reading (or hearing) the scriptures; before leading (or being led) in prayer; between the sentences and phrases as you preach (or listen to) the sermon. As you "pause, and pray," you can also deal with negative feelings—about self, a worship leader, a worshipper, a crying baby—infectiously changing the atmosphere!

I say this unapologetically for any who serve as lay readers, teachers, public speakers, counselors, or preachers: *It is surprising how people actually hear better with a few pregnant silences.* Over a decade ago, a patent attorney invited me to his home and gently taught me two practical truths: The *silences* in the sentences are as important as the words, and *repetition* is a key to good learning, as well as good liturgy.

Say something once—*pause, and pray inwardly,* then *repeat*—a quotation, a phrase, a question, a line from a story or a poem. How many times did Martin Luther King, Jr., repeat the refrain, "I have a dream"? ("Pause, and pray," works in conversing one-to-one or with groups.)

☐ Ignatius used an expression, *Non multa, sed multum,* "not many, but much," loosely translated, *Less is more*! It is a discipline of simplicity, a kind of fasting from words. Most ministers today were trained since the 1940s when churches began to broadcast on radio (then television) and followed the rubric: "No dead air space!" It is a demonic acculturation, a bad church habit that is hard to kick! No wonder the pace of Protestant worship generally gives little space for the worship leader, or the people, to listen for God to speak within. Fred Rogers of

"Mister Rogers' Neighborhood," an ordained Presbyterian minister, prophetically broke with television protocol, allowing silences while tying his shoes or waiting for a child to talk or tie her shoes.

● Work to get your church to allow pauses in the liturgy and incorporate at least one longer oasis of "Quaker silence"–indicated as *Silence for Personal Reflection and Prayer* or similar words–at an appropriate place. Or print the word *Silence* on a line after each Scripture reading. Sing the hymns as prayers; as your eyes greet another worshiper, let that glance become a visual prayer for God's best for that person; encourage the presence of children and humor while discouraging mere noisiness; interpret silences to children as "hush times" or times to focus on a favorite object.

If you lead worship, instead of standing immediately after the choir anthem, try sitting calmly and saying the Jesus Prayer or a verse of scripture as a "centering prayer." Then stand and walk prayerfully. Encourage people to think this way and print these ideas one by one in the bulletin from time to time.

● *The service of worship* is a fairly accurate equivalent for "liturgy" (Greek *leitourgia–laos + erga*), literally "the people's works." Invite people to express joys and concerns before the prayers of the people–out loud, briefly repeated by the worship leader for all to hear. Or for a large church, just allow space during the prayers and invite people to *whisper* aloud the first names of persons or brief concerns. Simply naming a concern aloud in the presence of God's people creates a powerful spiritual investment in worship. (Ask the choir and officers to help break the ice the first time.)

Folks come to our churches yearning for personal Transcendence in a computer age. Helping them to be comfortable with even brief silences in the service sets a corporate example: It encourages people to leaven their own liturgies or work, conversation, and play with contemplative pauses. Creating quiet Sabbath times to leaven the "service" is in itself a prophetic service, a counter-cultural witness against technology taking over the liturgies of our lives.

Hospitality: Extending the Lord's Table

The Lord's Supper dramatizes hospitality, pointing to Jesus' table-fellowship with outcasts. Benedict's words should be included as instructions to ushers, pastors, lay leaders, and church members:

> *Let all guests who arrive be received like Christ, for he is going to say, "I came as a guest, and you received me." And to all let due honor be shown. . . . In the reception of the poor and of pilgrims the greatest care and solicitude should be shown, because it is especially in them that Christ is received.*
> *—From the Rule of Saint Benedict*

☐ Hospitality and care for the needs of the *anawim*—physically handicapped, sight- and hearing-impaired persons, minorities, children, older adults, and visitors—will pay a direct dividend "in the *service* of worship." Hospitality by example creates a ripple effect of hospitality in people's homes and work.

● At a church growth seminar I heard a piece of research that contained an important piece of spirituality: *Most visitors or inactive members who show up in your congregation (except on high holy days!) have been going through a crisis.* I do not remember doing anything differently, but it changed my lens of perception and I discovered its truth. Visiting in homes, reading notes from the deacon's welcome phone call, even greeting at the door—I would become aware of a recent move, a career change, a family member in a nursing home, an infertile couple, a stillborn child, a lover's or a parent's crisis. After I learned it I knew it: The world breaks everyone. . . . Even a handshake at the door would become a prayer. We need to train our pastors and lay visitors and phone callers and people in the pews to listen through the Sunday impressions for the tips of these submerged crises. It would affect our prayers, our presence, and our programs.

A young adult tells how he dressed casually so that a poor father standing next to him would not feel inferior at the dedication service for this own child.[1]

● A simple gesture of hospitality from one person in the pew to another may be the bearer of a life-altering experience. In a powerful story in Victor Hugo's *Les Miserables,* young Marius is grieving the death of his father whom he never knew, having been separated from his father because of family disputes about the French Revolution. He returns to Saint Sulpice Church where his aunt had taken him as a child.

Being a bit more absent-minded than usual, kneeling down, he took his place behind a pillar, sitting without noticing on a chair bearing the inscription: *Monsieur Mabeuf, church warden.* No sooner had the service begun than an old man interrupted Marius: "Monsieur, this is my place." Marius moved over.

After Mass, as Marius was absorbed in thought, the old man spoke to him apologetically: He was sorry for having interrupted Marius, but it seemed the Mass was better from this seat; he preferred it to the bench, where he had a right to sit as warden. Why? Because years before, for ten years, he had watched "a poor, brave father" who had sat in this very chair. It seemed the man "had no other opportunity and no other way of seeing his child, being prevented through some family arrangements." The warden continued, describing the man:

> "He came at the hour when he knew his son was brought to mass. He looked at his child, and wept. This poor man worshipped this little boy. I saw that. This place has become sanctified, as it were, for me, and I have acquired the habit of coming here to hear the mass. . . . I was even acquainted slightly with this unfortunate gentleman. He had a father-in-law, a rich aunt, relatives, I do not remember exactly, who threatened to disinherit the child if he, the father, should see him. He had sacrificed himself that his son might some day be rich and happy. They were separated by political opinions. . . . He was one of Bonaparte's colonels. He is dead, I believe. He lived at Vernon . . . and his name is something like Pontmarie, Montpercy. He had a handsome sabre cut."
>
> "Pontmercy," said Marius, turning pale.
>
> "Exactly; Pontmercy. Did you know him?"
>
> "Monsieur," said Marius, "he was my father."
>
> The old churchwarden clasped his hands, and exclaimed, "Ah!

you are the child! Yes, that is it; he ought to be a man now. Well poor child, you can say that you had a father who loved you well."[2]

This is a "regenerative experience" for the young Marius—retroactive grace! A church warden's simple gesture of hospitality became a "service" of reconciliation for a man and his deceased father.

● People who visit our churches are starving for intimacy: "high tech, high touch" in this electronic world. Govans Presbyterian Church in Baltimore has reversed the normal declining membership statistics for city churches. They extend the Lord's Table by taking a loaf of fresh-baked bread to each new visitor. Bread is kept in the church freezer, heated, and delivered that very afternoon.

☐ *As we model prayer* we extend hospitality by motivating strugglers to pray. When verbal prayer is offered by an unlikely person—by one who is quiet or "uneducated" or by a respected person you might not think is "spiritual"—prayer serves as a magnetic force. A young pastor (seven feet tall!) took communion to a little aging woman in a nursing home. After his prayer, reaching up she touched him and offered a beautiful prayer *for him*! Where the hidden Christ is being formed in people, others will not feel pressured to pray: They will yearn to learn to yearn! One role model inspires others, "Teach us to pray. . . ."

Like "modeling clay," the examplary power of prayer in the lives of others molds us. Two African-Americans offer powerful contrasting examples of people who *modeled prayer*: One was a kataphatic prophet, Martin Luther King, Jr., who took on the whole world. The other was an apophatic mystic, Howard Thurman: "We keep a troubled vigil at the bedside of the world," he wrote. "Thus we clutch the moment of intimacy in worship when we become momentarily a part of a larger whole, a fleeting strength, which we pit against all the darkness and dread of other times."[3]

Communion itself by virtue of its being a radically simple meal *is modeling prayer*, making a statement that more is not always better, that there is joy in sacrifice, abundance in scarcity, beauty in simplicity.

Prayer itself *becomes* hospitality when we model the use of *inclusive language*. Before saying the Lord's Prayer, introduce it with scriptural images such as: "Like a mother who will never forget her nursing child, you taught us to pray the family prayer, 'Our Father . . . ' " or, "Like a woman who sweeps her house till she finds the lost coin, you invite us to pray boldly yet humbly, 'Our Father. . . . ' " Inclusive love mirrored in our language draws people to the real God, beyond our limited cultural images of God..

☐ There is a more profound meaning of hospitality: *Forgiveness is linked to the breaking of bread.* This is implied in the Pharisees' criticism of Jesus: "This fellow welcomes sinners and eats with them" (Luke 15:2). It is clear in Joseph's feeding and forgiveness of his extended family and former captors.

Forgiveness starts inside. Serving institutions too often think of service as fixing problems "out there." But unless we begin "in here" we cannot serve. The model of a forgiving community *is a thing of beauty in itself* and that becomes a powerful serving force.[4]

Forgiveness moves outside. The broken bread wordlessly shouts: "Forgive the world by feeding your enemy!" (Romans 12:20). The intensity of Christ's suffering is now celebrated as the intense joy of eucharist (Greek *eu-chara*), literally "good joy"! Christ's body offers up the intensity of the pain of the whole universe in hope "till Christ comes." Pascal says, "Jesus will be in agony until the end of the world, and we must not sleep until that time."

Simplify to Serve: Fasting as a Fundamental Attitude

The Lord's Supper by its simplicity is a summons to the Mystery of fasting and feasting. We feast on just a taste of pure joy but are never completely filled; the absence of abundance makes us yearn for more. "Blessed are those who hunger and thirst . . . " (Matthew 5:6).

The Sermon on the Mount, highlighting the silence of Jesus and the community, refers to fasting as *a normative discipline for believers*: "And whenever you fast, do not look dismal. . . . But when you fast, put oil on your face" (Matthew 6:16-17). It is not *if*, but *when* you fast.

☐ Fasting is an *inner spiritual attitude* outwardly manifested in simplicity of life, as the Quakers call it, or to use a phrase from my own Reformed heritage, moderation in all things. *The Random House*

Dictionary refers to fasting as "an ascetic discipline," from *askesis*, training. But training is never for its own sake but always for a purpose: Fasting is connected to vocation, *one's purpose for being on this earth.* Jesus pointed to this when the disciples urged him, "Rabbi, eat something" (John 4:31). He answered, "My food is to do the will of [the One] who sent me and to complete [that] work" (v. 34).

Periodic abstinence in one area of life gives a leaven of simplicity to the whole of life. We need occasional abstinence from even the good gifts of life, from food, reading, words, community, sex, work. The sabbath, the seventh day of creation, may be seen as fasting. Abstinence from outward activity is a gift so that we can contemplate the deeper, inward self.

☐ *Fasting is training for service.* But fasting itself can be prayer, and prayer can be service: "Prayer does not fit us for the greater work; prayer is the greater work," Oswald Chambers of the early YMCA movement would remind us in *My Utmost for His Highest.* Training for service, itself, can become a service. When I fast from words, I serve another by giving that person space to speak his or her own creative words; when I fast from my desire always to give ideas and things to others, I allow a space of grace to receive from another, thereby enhancing the divine dignity of another.

☐ Genuine fasting thus becomes a fundamental attitude toward life, a "set of the soul," *with important political as well as personal consequences.* When a "wealthy" nation fasts from its desire always to dictate to a "poor" nation how it must use technology, the "developed" nation allows the other nations to develop its creativity from the grass roots. Such corporate fasting leads to "appropriate technology": Laying small vinyl pipes for a "primitive" water system to keep people living in their native villages may be better than building only large reservoirs that attract people to cities, creating Third-World urban slums. By working *with* rather than doing *for* others, the guests may discover that they too are oppressed–rich in things and poor in soul–and may value the profound simple gifts of their hosts.

The words of Isaiah 58:6-8, often used for Ash Wednesday, express the positive social manifestation of any authentic fast:

Is not this the fast that I choose:
>   to loose the bonds of injustice,
>   to undo the thongs of the yoke,
> to let the oppressed go free,
>   and to break every yoke?
> Is it not to share your bread with the hungry,
>   and bring the homeless poor into your house;
> when you see the naked, to cover them,
>   and not to hide yourself from [neglect] your own kin?

PRAYER EXERCISE 34: A Youth Project—Bread for Bread

Have the youth of the church assemble on a Saturday night with enough supplies for baking approximately one loaf of bread for every five to ten worshippers. Incorporate this in an all-night "retreat," which may include singing, fellowship, and study. The bread baking begins and continues until all the loaves are baked. The fresh baked loaves may be wrapped then placed on wicker plate holders and set in the windows of the sanctuary.

When the Sunday morning congregation gathers, the aroma is still in the air. Use sentences concerning bread in the service: "I am the bread of life," and so forth. One of the youth makes an announcement (also printed in the newsletter and bulletin) indicating that the youth of the church baked the bread the previous night: "This is our gift to you and we invite you to take a loaf after the service and leave your gift for hungry people. Bread for bread; dough for dough."

PRAYER EXERCISE 35: Sacrificial Meal at Church or Home

For American Christians, a symbolic *sacrificial meal* may be the only reminder of fasting they will ever experience. At the beginning of Lent, some churches have a corporate meal of only soup and rice or bread and give out simple menus (and prayer litanies) to encourage

weekly sacrificial meals at home, using the saved money for hunger programs and the saved time for family prayer. This practice may encourage recycling of left-over food, paper, glass, and plastic throughout the year.

PRAYER EXERCISE 36: A Food Fast and Prayer

It is not hard to fast from some of our "luxuries." But because food is absolutely essential to life, every Christian would benefit from an actual food fast to feel the hunger and suffering of the very poor *as God's suffering* with them, and our hunger as *spiritual hunger*. It should be limited at first, such as a one-day juice fast or a rice-and-tea fast. But it is always fasting *and* prayer, with the intention to offer the fast as "prayer" for a person or cause and to open oneself more completely to God.

Simplify to Serve: Economy and *Oikoumene*

Our personal spiritual journey has led us to see the whole world as our home (*oikos*). The "cousin words" *economical* and *ecumenical* call us to simplify in order to serve. Concern for the well-being of the "the whole inhabited earth" (*oikonomia*) requires Christians to practice an *economy* toward material things, cultivating an attitude of simplicity. In the wisdom of the popular bumper sticker: *Live simply that others may simply live.*

An active lay leader in the world ecumenical movement early in this century, Robert E. Speer, gives the spiritual focus:

> Life is a great, worthy, holy, and divine thing. Life is to be used as a sacred trust. Life is to be a cup out of which thirsty men and women are to be given drink. Our lives are bread, by which hungry men and women are to be fed. We are in the world like our Master, not to be ministered unto, but to minister, and give our lives.[5]

Hildegard of Bingen speaks a word of urgency about economical living in our ecumenical age: "All of creation God gives to humankind to use. If this privilege is misused, God's justice permits creation to punish humanity." While scientists warn of further holes in the ozone layer and wetlands are threatened by concrete airports, through our praying we groan along with all creation for the glorious liberty of the children of God (Romans 8:18-28).

Fasting is a normative aspect of the imitation of Christ, *an attitude of cultivating sabbath spaces in our overcrowded lives.* Through this inward mindset, I participate in the silent self-emptying of Jesus the Mime, selectively keeping some of my best ideas below ground to gestate. Or, to use the above-ground metaphor, fasting means pruning the external vine so that I can become inwardly *generative and creative*—which is the discipline of vocation.

Theme 7
The Discipline of Vocation

CHAPTER XVIII

Generativity:
Bearing Fruits of Love

The root of faith bears fruit in our Lord Jesus Christ.

—Polycarp to the Philippians

What good is it to me if Mary gave birth to the son of God fourteen hundred years ago and I do not also give birth to the son of God in my time and in my culture? . . .The soul among all creatures is generative as God is.

—Meister Eckhart

Vocation is not what you do but who you are becoming. The highest reward for your toils is not what you get for it but what you become by it, to paraphrase John Ruskin. Classically, this is spiritual formation, the imitation of Christ.

The *discipline* of vocation is the quest for "a discerning mind and heart"—the prayer of the young King Solomon (1 Kings 3:5-12). The *discipline* of vocation involves discerning questions: How is God at work *in* me through all that is happening *around* me and *to* me? How is God inviting me to grow through *all* the experiences of my life–prodigal sins of my own fault; perfectionist sins of default, failing to claim my gifts out of fear; and circumstances beyond my control—for some meaningful purpose? Classically this is expressed in two ancient concepts of *providence* (God using all things for good purpose) and *mortification* of the flesh (little "dyings" that create new life in us).

Ironically, as when, in the aftermath of his greatest victory, Elijah asked to die (1 Kings 19), success as well as failure confronts us with the crucial vocational question: *What am I doing here?* The question is not, *What should I do?* but, *What am I living for?* Classically this is expressed as *discernment* of the will of God.

A *Why* to Live: My Purpose for Being on This Earth

Service includes work, so it may seem that this theme about vocation is unnecessary. *But our vocation is not our work.* Work itself may be a distraction from genuine community and serving. That is when one needs to ask, What am I working *for*?

Victor Frankl, in *Man's Search for Meaning*, described excruciating suffering in a death camp during the holocaust. Among people with identical circumstances of hunger, disease, and frostbite, he observed that most died. Yet some lived! As a psychiatrist, Frankl gave himself to studying these dynamics. Paraphrasing Nietzsche, he discovered that a person who has a *why* to live can survive almost any *how*.[1]

The *why* we are looking for transcends career. To identify vocation with work is to risk losing the core of your "self" if you "burn out," if the job becomes obsolete, if the economy goes into recession, when children leave home, when you retire from active career.

It is the question that ministers and all servant-leaders *need* to ask themselves, as Martha needed to ask it of her ministry: What is the *intent* behind the *content* of my serving? It is the question of retired persons and persons with disabilities: *What am I living for?* (see exercise 43.)

Discernment as Shema: A Call to Bliss and Blessing

Once you dedicate your life to service, then the question is *What form will that service take?* The *Shema* gives us our agenda again—*to listen* to what is happening in my life *and* in the world, *to discern* where God is at work in it, *to be attentive* to how God is inviting me. Freud said the purpose of life was "to love and to work." But what or whom do you love? And what cause are you working for? Hitler was in love with his own demonic dream and addicted to his own work to accomplish it.

Joseph Campbell expresses it as *following your bliss*. People misquote Campbell's phrase, referring to *finding* your bliss. But it is *follow*, not find. *Follow* is a discipleship word. Bliss is not an end in itself; it is not a cheap grace to justify sexual violence or promiscuity, environmental plundering, or a narcissistic lifestyle—"if it feels good, do it." The word *bliss* is related to "blessing," and genuine blessing embraces self *and* others. Let's consider several qualities of bliss.

☐ *There is no genuine bliss for self unless it results in blessing for others.* Discernment is not finding what is best for *me* but following what is best for *myself in relation to others. Following* calls for discipline in living out my bliss. If we split bliss from blessing it becomes a curse: Hitler was not following his bliss but his curse. "Do you create or do you destroy?" Hammarskjold would ask us in his *Markings.*

In a TV program on hatred, hosted by Bill Moyers, young gang members described how killing another gang member gave them a tremendous "high." But the addict's high does not arise out of bliss but from demonic fear and self-doubt. Yet even a ruined high can become an awe-ful vacuum to beckon a person to the Most High. It still happens.

We are called to return to the *Shema, listening* from below, a call to wholeness and holiness. It is your *original* blessing, unique to you, as we might say, "That is an original piece of work." My bliss is not your bliss. Follow *your* bliss.

☐ *Individual bliss severed from communal blessing is narcissism.* Like its Greek namesake Narcissus, narcissism begins with self-infatuation but ends in self-destruction. Dis-obedience, literally inattentiveness, is dangerous; it is living counter to *shema.* Not to delight in God is to miss the desires of one's own heart; it is the wide gate and easy road, *the undiscerned path,* that leads to destruction (Psalm 37:4; Matthew 7:13). It is to be tricked by attachments that ultimately deceive, "like chaff that the wind drives away" (Psalm 1:4). Sin is *whatever distorts our original blessing* by telling us to live by others' expectations instead of following our own original bliss and blessing.

By contrast, "those who delight in God" will be "like trees . . . which yield their fruit in its season" (Psalm 1:3). The word *delight* in the Psalms is equivalent to *contemplation.* An outward vocational crisis can be a manifestation of an inward crisis in contemplation. A vocational emergency is an opportunity for spiritual emergence.

So there is good news! The "crisis" in our Lord's life is portrayed in John's gospel as Jesus being "lifted up" (John 3:14, 8:28). Any "cross" we encounter becomes a creative occasion to "rise above" crisis! Every crisis is a summons to *shema.* Even our vocational mirages, false starts, and negative circumstances, *if surrendered to God,* can retroactively draw us to our bliss and become a source of blessing. We are *Christianoi,* "little Christ's," little "anointed ones" (Acts 11:26), but it is anointing silhouetted by affliction: "Blessed are the poor in spirit."

☐ Following your bliss is *a lifelong process of discernment:* "Go . . . . and I will bless you . . . so that you will be a blessing" (Genesis 12:1-3). God still calls aging Abrahams and Sarahs. People are launching second careers; many are living as long after retirement as they spent "working." The person having a "why" to live finds meaning long after children leave home, health or business fails, or relationships end in death or divorce.

In restating the two great commands from the Torah, to love God and neighbor, Jesus said nothing new. What *is* unique in the gospel portraits is that *Jesus actually lived out this union of contemplating God's love and manifesting love to others.* His life *was* his message. There is no gap between *contemplation,* Jesus' deep gladness, and its appropriate outward *manifestation,* connecting with the world's deep hunger: "A good devout person first arranges inwardly the things to be done outwardly," writes Thomas a Kempis in *The Imitation of Christ.*

In those moments when *contemplation becomes manifestation,* we are actually energized through our *interaction* with the world: "My food is to do the will of the one who sent me" (John 4:34). The tree is not nurtured directly from the elements transmitted through the roots, *but by their interaction with the world:* Through the process of spiritual photosynthesis the roots of faith develop fruits of love. Such occasions of genuine vocational energy become Christ's work in us: "Work out your own salvation . . . for it is God who is at work in you" (Philippians 2:12-13). In *Work and Contemplation,* Douglas Steere expresses the goal of Quaker spirituality: "For there is a point where, blasphemous as it may sound, the contemplator is always at prayer and where [one] is free to carry [one's] action into the contemplation and the contemplation into the action. . . . It is, in short, *an abiding disposition,* and out of this the works come."[2]

When these two come together, we have returned to home, to "Eden," to our original bliss and blessing. Creative "genius" personalities *love* what they do, taking a childlike delight in painting, composing, or searching for a grand theory of the universe. They wed the most advanced ideas in their field to the wonder-filled attitude of a child.[3] And that childlikeness is our "call"!

Generativity as Original Blessing: Sex and Work

To *contemplate* the deep gladness of your first love—"You are precious in my sight"—is to know your "original blessing" (Matthew Fox). To *manifest* it is to "follow your bliss" (Joseph Campbell).

The mark of this blessing is generativity *with* responsibility: "So God created humankind in [God's] image . . . male and female [God] created them. God blessed them, and God said to them, 'Be fruitful and multiply . . . and have dominion [custodianship, responsibility] . . . over every living thing' . . . and indeed, it was very good" (Genesis 1:27-28, 31). So in the first account of creation (1:1-2:4a) generativity *and* responsibility are fused together as blessing: *Be creative and take care of creation.*

In the second account (2:4b-25), we see the same *at-one-ment* between responsibility *and* generativity: "The Lord God took the man and put him in the garden to Eden to till it and to keep it" (2:15); "A man leaves his father and his mother and clings to his wife, and they become one flesh. And the man and his wife were both naked, and were not ashamed" (2:24-25).

Before any mention of sin in the world, sex *and* work are created as *good gifts!* I remember my ecstasy the summer I was learning Hebrew and translated these texts, as if reading them for the first time! In my youth I was given negative attitudes about sex and more than my share of a Calvin-*ist* work ethic. Yet Calvin himself broke with medieval tradition and "protested" that *sexuality is for re-creative as well as procreative purposes*; and that *work is meant as a gift, not a curse*. I now think of myself as *Calvinian*, as later Calvin-*ists* became negative![4] Our original blessing celebrates the union of sexuality with vocation.

Sex *and* work are both blessed in Genesis 1 and 2. Be generative *and* responsible. Be fruitful *and* take care. But the result of the "fall" that happens to each of us (Genesis 3 onward) is that work degenerates to drudgery: "By the sweat of your face / you shall eat bread." Sex degenerates to exploitation: "and he shall rule over you" (3:19, 16). With a backdrop of drudgery and exploitation as the cultural norms, Jesus' Gospel is counter-cultural, "but from the beginning it was not so" (Matthew 19:8). The mystery of Christ inaugurates the "new Genesis," a new beginning (Colossians 1:15-20). "So if anyone is in Christ, there is a new creation" (2 Corinthians 5:17)!

Our being created in the divine image and restored through Christ succinctly states our calling: *to discern, day by day, how best to reflect our original blessing to all creation by being fruitful, creative, and generative.*

Genesis and Generativity: Sexuality and Spirituality

The command to be fruitful and multiply runs throughout scripture, but it means far more than biological reproduction. It is spiritual generativity, being fruitful in love: "They are like trees . . . which yield their fruit in its season" (Psalm 1:3). "The righteous flourish like the palm tree. . . . / In old age they still produce fruit" (Psalm 92:12, 14). "The fruit of righteousness will be peace" (Isaiah 32:17 NIV). "You will know them by their fruits" (Matthew 7:20). "I am the vine, you are the branches. Those who abide in me and I in them bear much fruit" (John 15:5). "Asking that you may be filled with the knowledge of God's will . . . as you bear fruit in every good work" (Colossians 1:9-10). "The fruit of the Spirit is love, joy, peace, patience, kindness, generosity, faithfulness, gentleness, and self-control" (Galatians 5:22-23). "Now, discipline always seems painful rather than pleasant at the time, but later it yields the peaceful fruit of righteousness . . . " (Hebrews 12:11). "On either side of the river, is the tree of life with its twelve kinds of fruit . . . and the leaves of the tree are for the healing of the nations" (Revelation 22:2).

☐ From Genesis to Revelation, the theme of generativity is celebrated as a primary mark of our original blessing in *creation* and a sign of our *re-creation* in Christ through the Spirit, "fecundity" as Henri Nouwen describes it in *Lifesigns.* The tree in the Garden of Eden, linked with sexuality, is now the tree of life in the celestial city—its fruitfulness sublimated not only for healing of individuals, *but for the healing of the nations!* One thinks of Gandhi, fasting from intimacy with his wife, but creating eternal intimacy with all India and humankind.

☐ The theme of generativity continues *down through the centuries in the writings of ascetic theologians,* for whom sexuality has always been a primary paradigm of the mystical union of Christ. God is described as a birther: "What does God do all day long? God gives birth," wrote Meister Eckhart. "I am in love and my bride is called poverty. No one has been anxious to woo her since Jesus lived," said Francis of Assisi. The maverick Japanese Christian mystic and social activist Toyohiko Kagawa survived by praying:

Oh Eternal bosom, poured out from God . . .
It is the best nourishment for a lonely orphan,
for a sulking and twisted soul like mine,
indeed food for my soul.
Mother's bosom is God's bosom.[5]

Your original blessing is restored as you die and rise with Christ: You re-present the creative generativity of God in a unique way in the world.[6] John Magee writes, "Prayer is identification with the creativity of God. . . . It is living at the growing edge of the universe, those living nodal points where the future is coming into existence."[7]

☐ The relationship between sexuality and spirituality follows *the pattern of Mary*, the church giving birth to Christ in the life of the believing community. Mary's example of listening obedience (Luke 1:38) and contemplative pondering (Luke 2:19, 51) is the seedbed for the Word to be reproduced in the world: "We give birth to [Christ] through our holy works which ought to shine on others by our example," said Francis of Assisi. In *Gandhi's Truth,* Erik Erickson wrote, "The true saints are those who transfer the state of householdership to the house of God, becoming father and mother, brother and sister, son and daughter, to all creation, rather than to their own issue."[8] "Whoever does the will of [Abba] is my brother and sister and mother," said Jesus (Matthew 12:50).

The intricate connection of our human sexuality and our spiritual generativity is both frightening *and* exhilarating. It is the "terrific thing," "terrific" as in wonderful, yet also "terrifying."[9] We can be liberated by Christ or enslaved by demons. As Rollo May pointed out in *Love and Will*, the *daemon* is the creative force within us, susceptible to good or evil. This intricate sexual-spiritual connection carries with it the awesome potential represented by "the tree of life" in Genesis, the *yetzer ha tov* and *the yetzer ha ra*, the good tendency and the evil tendency. Only through the process of mortification is the "terrific thing" of this *daemon* freed yet also disciplined as a positive life-force for self and others.

Biblically, the "terrific thing" of our sexuality *and* spirituality is expressed as generativity. It is not merely *biological* but *incarnational* generativity, uniting the spiritual and the material. For some, generativity *is* primarily biological. For Anna Maria Pertl and Leopold Mozart, despite each parent's own talents, their generativity was chiefly embodied in giving the world the biological prodigy of Wolfgang Amadeus. But for Amadeus, the "terrific thing" of his generativity was incarnated in his sublime music! However, biological fruitfulness can also be sublimated into other far-reaching gifts.

● Sexual imagery has been used in many *hymns* to express the sweetness of communion with the Lord, as in this classic by Bernard of Clairvaux: "Jesus, the very thought of Thee With sweetness fills my breast, But sweeter far Thy face to see And in Thy presence rest."

As a metaphor of the believer's union with Christ, Bernard, like John of the Cross and others, was drawn to the romantic ecstasy in the Song of Solomon, which was probably written *simply as a love song*. Yet, with countless Christian *and* Jewish mystics, we can appreciate the obvious parallels between sexual and spiritual romance.

Such hymns have been all but eliminated from most hymnals but are still regularly requested in nursing homes. C. Austin Miles' "In the Garden" is a favorite: "I come to the garden alone, While the dew is still on the roses. . .And the joy we share as we tarry there, None other has ever known." Through spiritual intimacy with Jesus, many women, and men as well, have found positive sublimation for an emptied marriage, a boring job, or codependent relationships, intimacy that allowed them to go on living and loving with hope.

● The place for the training of ministers, theological *seminary*, means the "seedbed" where the seeds of faith will germinate and bear fruit. And while "seminary" is a male symbol, a primary symbol in every local church is feminine: The baptismal font represents *the womb* as the church becomes the place where Christ is born again and again in its members.

● One more spiritual-sexual connection: In Hebrew and Greek the same verb for *knowing* is used to refer to spiritual *and* sexual intimacy. "Now the man *knew* his wife Eve, and she conceived and bore Cain" (Genesis 4:1). "Be still and *know* . . . " (Psalm 46:10). "I want *to know* Christ and the power of his resurrection and the sharing of his sufferings by becoming like him" (Philippians 3:10).

● The idea of generativity comes right out of my own *Calvinian roots,* from the Westminster Catechisms and longer Confession where *regeneration* is used to describe the new life. Regenerative experiences are rooted in Re-formation and "catholic" tradition.

☐ What creates *the experiential connection* between sexuality and spirituality, our original blessing in creation and our need for redemption through the cross? For John of the Cross the key is *self-forgetting love:*

> One dark night,
> Fired with love's urgent longings
> —Ah, the sheer grace!—
> I went out unseen,
> My house being now all stilled . . .
>
> I abandoned and forgot myself
> Laying my face on my beloved;
> All things ceased; I went out from myself,
> Leaving my cares
> Forgotten among the lilies.

Ironically, the "sheep" of Matthew 25 *forgot themselves*, unaware that in loving the very least they were loving Jesus. In a moment of altruism the self-conscious ego dies: "He wounded my neck / With his gentle hand / Suspending all my senses."[10] In acts of genuine altruism endorphins are released akin to the experience of orgasm, which in

French is *le petit mort,* "the little death." And *blesser* means "to bless" but also "to wound": Jacob is blessed *and* wounded. Our spiritual conception begins with self-emptying.

Your Vocation:
"Turn Everything to Your Advantage"

It is clear why a primary word for spiritual "discipline" is *gymnastikos*: "training" requires me to become spiritually "naked" (*gymnos*). Living out my baptism, I die with Christ, stripped "naked" like the youth in Mark 14:52. Then I rise to put on the new clothing of compassion and love (Mark 16:5-8; Colossians 3:1-17).[11] Divesting my attachments, I embrace my vulnerabilities and so become spiritually resilient.

As Thomas à Kempis writes in *The Imitation,* "Turn everything to your advantage;" he, of course, means spiritually. That is our vocation: to embrace the suffering of our lives and of the world, then offer it as participation in the divine cosmic birthpangs transforming adversity to advantage. "Mortification" is a *process* of putting to death our short-lived attachments to put on the lasting values of our resurrection existence. Even retroactively, our sexual, physical, and psychic woundings can become painful doorways to strength and new life.

PRAYER EXERCISE 37: Chant: Turn to God in All Things

The words of this chant echo thoughts expressed by Mechtild of Magdeburg and countless mystics throughout the ages. Use the chant to help you pray all of life's circumstances:

Turn to God in all things, in all things see God.

Turn to God in All Things
A Chant

Kent Ira Groff, 1991
Adapted from Mechtild of Magdeburg

Kent Ira Groff, 1991
arr. J. M. Seefeldt, 1993

(repeat as desired)

CHAPTER XIX

Mortification: Painful Prunings

Blackberry winter, the time when the hoarfrost lies on the blackberry blossoms; without this frost the berries will not set. It is the forerunner of a rich harvest.

— Margaret Mead, *Blackberry Winter*

Paradoxically, the way to restore the generativity of our original blessing is through dying. This is the meaning of "mortification of the flesh": an active surrendering of this-worldly experiences of failure *and* success. It is to take up the cross: The paschal *mystery*–new birth through dying to self. Margaret Mead captured the Mystery in the image of *Blackberry Winter* where the hoarfrost is the forerunner of a rich harvest.

Suffering as Birthpangs: Dying to New Life

Jesus' words crystallize the mystery: "I tell you, unless a grain of wheat falls into the earth and dies, it remains just a single grain; but if it dies, it bears much fruit" (John 12:24).

Mortification is the mystery of how emptiness can lead to fulfillment, how self-denial is the door to self-realization and generativity. It is the strange mystery that *kenosis* is the prelude to *pleroma*: The *emptied* Christ is now the *fullness* of God (Philippians 2; Colossians 1-2). This gives an existential meaning to the historical tradition of the empty tomb: In returning and embracing their sadness, women, and then men, encounter the joyous Presence of the risen Lord! The emptiness of the dark, underground silence is just what the roots of faith need to thrive and be-come generative again. The darkness of the "womb" births the spiritual quality of "compassion," both words from the Hebrew root *raham*.

Joy awaits when we embrace the emptiness of the tomb,
Ecstatic pain—com-passion bursting from the womb.

It is no coincidence that a primary biblical metaphor integrating
sexuality and spirituality is the image of suffering *as spiritual birthpangs*. The sexual image of birthpangs is a biblical metaphor uniting
"crucial" suffering and "resurrection" ecstasy in the believer's spiritual
experience: The pain of dying to self leads to new birth and union in
Christ.

☐ These birthpangs have *personal* significance, providing a powerful metaphor of the paschal mystery:

When a woman is in labor, she has pain, because her hour has
come. But when her child is born, she no longer remembers the
anguish because of the joy of having brought a human being into
the world. So you have pain now; but I will see you again, and
your hearts will rejoice. . . . Ask and you will receive, so that your
joy may be complete (John 16:20-24).

☐ The birthpangs have *interpersonal* significance, offering a spiritual perspective to painful conflict—even church conflict. Paul wrote to
the church in Galatia: "My little children, for whom I am again in the
pain of childbirth until Christ is formed in you" (Galatians 4:19).

☐ The birthpangs on all these levels are part of a divine *political
and cosmic* process of redemption: "For nation will rise against nation,
and kingdom against kingdom; there will be earthquakes in various
places; there will be famines. This is but the beginning of the birthpangs" (Mark 13:8). "We know that the whole creation has been groan-
ing in labor pains until now" (Romans 8:22).

In these texts, as throughout the Bible, *the experiential link that
transforms suffering into creative birthpangs is prayer*: "Ask and you
will receive, so that your joy may be complete" (John 16:24, see 16:22).

And not only the creation, but we ourselves . . . groan inwardly. . . .
for we do not know how to pray as we ought, but that very Spirit
intercedes with *sighs [groans, breathings]* too deep for words. And

God, who searches the heart, knows what is the mind of the Spirit, because the Spirit intercedes for the saints *according to the will of God.* We know that all things work together for good for those who love God, who are called according to [God's] *purpose* (Romans 8:23, 26-28, italics added).

A mother pointed out to me that the two themes of these verses parallel the experience of physical childbirth: Paying attention to *simp le breathing* (8:26), while at the same time paying attention to *the ultimate purpose* (8:28), birthing a child, makes the pain bearable *and* meaningful.

These two physical experiences, *breathing and ultimate purpose,* have spiritual parallels in exercise 8, "Breathing as Prayer" (and 38, below), and exercise 43, "My Life Mission Statement."

Continuous prayer of surrender is the existential link so that suffering takes on a sense of meaning and purpose This deep purpose is what we mean by "vocation." Nothing is more helpful for continuous surrender than "the prayer of the heart."

PRAYER EXERCISE 38: The Prayer of the Heart

"The prayer of the heart" is an ancient practice to encourage praying constantly, moment by moment, as naturally as breathing:

> (inhaling, receiving) *O Lord Jesus Christ, [Son of God],*
> (holding, cleansing)
> (exhaling, surrendering) *have mercy on me [a sinner].*

So the prayer begins "to pray itself," even when one is not consciously repeating the words. (See the form of "receiving, cleansing, giving" in exercise 8.)

Spiritual formation needs repetition. Repeated use of the Jesus Prayer or other centering prayer acts like a "rock polisher," cycling around and around until our rough churnings become a thing of beauty.

Mortification and Generativity: Pruning and Fecundity

"I am the true vine, and my Father is the vine grower. [God] removes every branch in me that bears no fruit. Every branch that bears fruit [God] prunes to make it bear more fruit" (John 15:1-2).

The biblical metaphor of "pruning" expresses the mystery, *how mortification leads to new life.* Like two siblings from a broken home, psychology and spirituality have too long been separated. Urban T. Holmes, III, related ascetic theology to the insights of psychology: "We cannot always 'celebrate growth.' Mortification refers to that intentional action of pruning of life that better life might grow by God's grace—just as better roses grow by God's grace."[1] Holmes's life was "cut short," yet it is still bearing fruit.

The horticultural image of mortification makes good psychological sense: A life without significant sacrifice also lacks courageous action. Last year I neglected to prune our lilacs; this year they bore few blooms. Pruning is a metaphor of the mystery of the Christ-life: leading by serving, self-fulfillment through self-surrender. Less *can* be more.

My forestry consultant friend says there are two ways to renew growth in trees: One is fertilizing the root system, below ground. The other is intentional pruning of the visible life, not only dead wood, but living wood, a process that stimulates growth *both above and below ground.* Here is a demonstrable, scientific paradox.

Simply put: *Pruning can be an alternative to fertilizer!* In "developed" societies, we have accepted the artificial fertilizer assumption, environmentally and spiritually. We have neglected to recognize that pruning our lives and institutions is an alternative to injecting more technological growth-agents into our internal systems. In the Greek of John 15, one word is used for the two English words *pruning* and *purging*: *Pruning purges us.* Pruning is simply the long-term net gain of intentional fasting from an overabundance of things, words, sex, intellectualism, money, food, busyness, and possessions.

Mortification and Suffering:
Surrender versus Resignation

Mortification has two sides: the *intentional* pruning and the *unintentional* purging that life deals us through outward circumstances that we would not choose, which can also become a means of growth.

☐ Mortification is the cultivation of *an attitude* of daily dying and rising to new life with Christ. It is practicing a baptismal lifestyle. It is character formation, learning to use negative experiences to find meaning and purpose, like a chain reaction: "knowing that suffering produces endurance, and endurance produces character, and character produces hope, and hope does not disappoint us" (Romans 5:3-4).

Prayer gets the ground ready. It is the cultivation of genuine humility, which makes positive use of life's humus: holy humus! Taking the lead from Luther's visceral spirituality, we might aptly find new meaning in the expression "holy shit!" Maybe people are "praying" without knowing it when they say it, unconsciously yearning that even life's waste might be consecrated, used for wholeness and holiness. *Consecrated waste becomes holy*, contributing to personal and cosmic wholeness.

Genuine humility is the learned art of a person whose character develops the consistent ability to deflect and transform negative experiences into growth. "It is silent, inconspicuous, dark and yet it is always ready to receive any seed, ready to give it substance and life. The more lowly, the more fruitful. . . . In that position, nothing can shatter the soul's serenity, its peace and joy," Anthony Bloom writes in *Living Prayer*.

This attitude of humility is like an inner "set of the sail" that comes from daily practice of dying to new life, and it can help us to deal with *the unintentional winds of affliction*. One of my students lives with a chronic, demyelinating illness; she is my teacher: "Acceptance differs from resignation which can engender bitterness and negative energy. Surrender admits and accepts the limitation and offers it as a positive dimension of the life wholly lived. . . . God transforms the affliction and suffering but does not bypass it."[2]

☐ Mortification is not *resignation* but *surrender*: offering all kinds of affliction—personal failure or tragic circumstances, which in the case of illness is failure of one's physical systems—as nurturing humus for new life. Religion that "manipulates" God and promises eutopia betrays the pattern of the Servant-Lord—"Your will be done. . . . Into your hands I commend my spirit." In the end it leaves one totally unprepared to face creatively the tragic surprises and even successes of life.

Mortification and Re-Generativity: The Joseph Story

Our vocation is one of continuous listening; we can never go beyond the *Shema*: How is God inviting me through this experience of difficulty? Of accomplishment?

The story of Joseph (Genesis 37-50)—sold by his brothers into slavery in Egypt, then rising to become the "lord" in charge of world relief—weaves together the themes of *mortification and regenerativity, sexuality and vocation, humility and comedy, hospitality and forgiveness, in a powerful summation of providence:* "Even though you intended to do harm to me, God intended it for good" (Genesis 50:20).

Yet Joseph did not reach the state of equanimity and sublime use of tragedy immediately or without pain. Tears and solitude, fasting and jesting, tantalizing his brothers while remaining anonymous, returning money in their sacks, putting the cup in Benjamin's sack, are some of the creative methods Joseph used to deal with years of anger.

Joseph's solitude, practiced well during years of imprisonment, has prepared him as he grieved his way toward manifestation and disclosure: "I am your brother, Joseph, whom you sold into Egypt. And now do not be distressed, or angry with yourselves, because you sold me here; for God sent me before you to preserve life" (Genesis 45:4-5).

Providence: Personal *and* Social Trans-Formation

Joseph's saga is a model of the creative yet honest movement through grieving and longing to believing and belonging. The story illustrates Providence by integrating personal, interpersonal, political, and cosmic

---

suffering, ecological disaster and famine, family and international injustice, with sexual abuse, e.g., Judah's incest with Tamar (Genesis 38) in contrast to Joseph's sexual discipline (Genesis 39). This creative movement unfolds only over time. Sibling rivalry, disillusioned dreams, and honest anger are sublimated into hospitality, laced with comedy as a tool of divine justice. Food becomes a sensual, kataphatic manifestation of forgiveness.

Finally, the brothers and Joseph must grieve again after their father Jacob dies: "Then [Joseph's] brothers also wept," asking forgiveness again, and "Joseph wept when they spoke to him" (50:17-18). Joseph is now humbled, his youthful, narcissistic dreams tempered—"Am I in the place of God?" (50:19). All these ingredients pave the long, long road toward seeing the hand of Providence, weaving creative vocation out of tragedy: "As for you, you meant evil against me, but God meant it for good, [so] that many people should be kept alive, as they are today. So do not fear; I will provide for you and your little ones" (50:20-21 RSV).

☐ Joseph's story represents the heart of Christian vocation: Personal character formation and forgiveness are linked with outward social transformation. Joseph embodies the unity of the Hebrew Bible and the New Testament, foreshadowing the pattern of the Messiah whose own mortification becomes the door to new life. It is a powerful example of the *protoevangelion*, the "pre-gospel" in "Genesis," a message of redemption and continuing "generativity."

Here is providence: *God's good gifts of creation are violated.* Sex is exploited through dysfunctional family and political structures. Work is desecrated as punitive slavery. *Yet all is used for a vocation, part of a cosmic, divine purpose, the earliest recorded world hunger program!*

☐ The Joseph saga prefigures the paschal mystery of the Christ *incognito*: Wherever pain and suffering are silently offered up and transformed into new life and purpose, *the hidden Christ is silently at work.* People experience "regenerative moments," yet only years later associate these with the name of Christ. In a moment when the hidden Presence transforms human futility into birthing labor pains, Christ is present: The rock in the desert "was Christ"; Moses "suffered for Christ."[3]

● Joseph expresses our third path by integrating the use of the world's creative gifts and what Teilhard called "the passive diminishments of affliction": Joseph's self-centered sensual dreams *and* later tragic circumstances give birth to vocation. "Christian" vocation transforms the world's brokenness into blessing: *generativity* (Erikson), *meaning* (Frankl), *self-actualization* (Maslow): You get involved in a cause outside your own skin, working at something very precious to you, "some calling or vocation in the old sense, the priestly sense, so that the work-joy dichotomy disappears."[4]

● In the dying-rising Christ, the deep Joy hidden at the heart of our suffering existence, entered history: "The [M]ystery hidden for ages" continues to transform the real stuff of human existence (Ephesians 3:9). When reporters asked Walker Percy why there were so many good Southern writers, he said, "Because we lost the War." Contemplate this Mystery the next time you hear jazz, a unique art form born out of demonic violence against slaves. An African-American gospel singer expressed it: "I do my best singing when I'm really burdened down." It is Maya Angelou's message in *I Know Why the Caged Bird Sings.* Here is the Mystery: "My grace is sufficient for you, for my power is made perfect in weakness" (2 Corinthians 12:9).

PRAYER EXERCISE 39: Gifts in Strengths and Weaknesses

Read 2 Corinthians 12:6-10. Contemplate the Mystery *in your life*: Identify one strength at a time and ponder how it also contains a weakness Then meditate on weaknesses and see what gift each one also contains.

Vocation: Forgiveness Manifested as Hospitality

One of the most powerful features at the end of Joseph's story is the connection between *hospitality and forgiveness.* The inward grace of forgiving his brothers is manifested in the outward fruit of Joseph's hospitality. The connection between forgiveness and food is clearly seen in Jesus' table fellowship with outcasts. It is Paul's teaching: "If your enemies are hungry, feed them" (Romans 12:20).

Such high-risk hospitality is our "giving back." It is my debt of gratitude: "Forgiveness, therefore, always entails a sacrifice. The price you must pay for your own liberation through another's sacrifice is that you in turn must be willing to liberate in the same way, irrespective of the consequences to yourself," wrote Hammarskjold.[5] Only *surrendered* failure becomes nurturing "humus." One of the greatest failures I need to surrender is my failure to forgive, or the failure of others to forgive me.

One of the most difficult barriers to vocational clearness is *the wound of unforgiveness.* Robert Bly's insight in *Iron John* especially applies to men, but is true for all. "The paradoxical teaching that where a person's wound is, that is where one's genius will likely be . . . that is precisely the place for which we will give our major gift to the community."[6]

The key to Joseph's resiliency is *surrender through forgiveness— manifested in hospitality.* What if Joseph had never met his brothers again? Forgiveness is different where reconciliation is impossible. I invite you to a simple releasing exercise, which over time can clear one's inner vision.

PRAYER EXERCISE 40: Meditating on Forgiveness

If you are experiencing pain in a relationship—with a child, spouse, friend, or co-worker—*visualize Jesus on the cross sharing the pain that* you *feel in that relationship* (see exercise 3). If there are persons *you* cannot forgive, open your arms outward and, in rhythm to your breathing, feel *Christ* praying in you: *Abba, forgive them, for they do not know what they are doing.*

Robert Coles tells of the African-American Ruby Bridges as a child on her way to a white school in New Orleans in the sixties, walking through lines of angry white people, her lips moving. He discovered what she was saying: "Father, forgive them, because they do not know . . . ." *Forgiveness is a doorway to courage.* It is also honest praying: Humanly *I* cannot forgive; only Christ can. "Unrepentant" people do *not* know what they are doing; they *think* they are hurting you (they are), *but they hurt themselves far more.* For an extended experience try to spend a few minutes with this exercise several days a week for about a month.

PRAYER EXERCISE 41: Lunch with a Disagreeable Person

Carl Jung noted that people who irritate us frequently remind us of a part of the self that we do not like. This gives new meaning to Jesus' words, "Love your enemy," because when we do, we embrace an alien part of ourselves and become more whole! Here is a prayer of "manifestation": Invite someone out to eat who "rubs you the wrong way." Prayerfully, be attentive to anything God may be teaching you about some silent part of you that you need to embrace.

Sexuality and Work: Celebrated *and* Disciplined

Through our vocation, *who we are* and *what we do* come together to form our *identity* in Christ. This is true re-formation. It is the strange paradox that our work is something we do yet it is only a manifestation of God's work in us, expressed in the Latin koan, *orare est laborare est orare* [to pray is to work is to pray]. "Work out your own salvation . . . for it is God who is at work in you" (Philippians 2:12-13).

☐ Vocation means discerning a way through one's "calling"—and "answering"—to glorify God by serving others. Inward contemplation of the Mystery of how deeply I am loved manifests itself through my outward life and work. Actually, in the end the providence of God is manifested to Joseph's family *only* through the providence of Joseph: "I myself will provide for you and your little ones" (Genesis 50:21). As George Eliot wrote,

> 'Tis God gives skill,
> But not without [human] hands:
> [God] could not make
> Antonio Stradivari's violins
> Without Antonio.

It is always *being* first, then *doing*. If evangelical and re-formed Christians are true to the best of the Puritan and Reformed heritage, neither *sexuality* nor *work* will be condemned, but rather *celebrated* and at the same time *disciplined*. Work, like sex, is a blessing that can become an addiction and needs to be disciplined. "Sabbath" is the discipline of contemplation when even God limits Godself: Generativity is restored by ceasing all activity, in order to contemplate, fasting from work to bask in the glow of creation!

☐ Christian vocation can be a unity of *both disciplined lifestyle* ("Catholic" value of celibate denial) and *fruitful work* ("Reformed" value of secular involvement), not just for religious and clergy, but for *all* ordinary Christians. The key to the third, transformative, path is *mortification*: offering all of life to God, its blessings and curses, as nurturing humus. Weaknesses become a source of strength: that is the *discipline* of vocation. *Meaningful doing flows from the formation of discerning character.*

● In the Torah God calls; in the Psalms we answer: "I delight to do your will, O my God; / your [Torah] is within my heart" (Psalm 40:8, see Hebrews 10:7). Our "job" is to discern the signals and "return the call" *in all circumstances* illustrated by all the moods and situations of the Psalms.

All of our thinking, speaking, and acting is merely "answering speech." It is what Quaker founder George Fox meant: "Go cheerfully about the world, *answering* to that of God in every one." John Anderson, director of Pendle Hill, the Quaker center near Philadelphia, confided that he used to say, " . . . *speaking* to that of God in every one," until an older Friend gently chided him that Fox had said "*answering* to that of God"—which first requires *listening*!

● We are back to the *Shema* as the organizing principle of the whole spiritual life, attentiveness to *the call to re-turn* our gaze to our first Love: "You are precious in my sight"; attentiveness to *the call to cele-brate* that love: "you shall love the Lord your God with all your heart . . . "; and attentiveness to *the call to the long obedience*: "You shall love your neighbor as yourself." Answering to that of God in every person is a lifelong process of discernment.

CHAPTER XX

Discernment: A Lifelong Call

The place God calls you to is the place where your deep gladness and the world's deep hunger meet.

— Frederick Buechner, *Wishful Thinking*

To what are we to be consecrated? Not to Christian work, but to the will of God to be and do whatever [God] requires.

— Watchman Nee, *The Normal Christian Life*

Your vocation is to continually discern from within your "being" what God is calling you to be "doing" in each new circumstance and chapter of your life. "Discernment" implies a continuing process, illustrated by one of its Greek roots. *Diakrisis* literally means "*through* crisis," and *diakrino* means "to judge or decide *through*." Most major turning points in life come to us via *crisis*. "Through" implies a process where the Spirit has been at work in us over time, whereas "decision" reflects an act of will at a point in time. Good decisions are the "ripened fruit" of a process of discernment.

Discernment—of the Will of God

"Do not be conformed to this world, but be transformed by the renewing of your minds, so that you may discern what is the will of God—what is good and acceptable and perfect" (Romans 12:2).

If you look up *discernment* in a Catholic library or periodical index, you find lots of literature. But there's relatively little on the subject in Protestant publications. Yet Protestants have written lots about "the will of God."[1] What we are really speaking about is the complete phrase, *discernment of the will of God*, as the text in Romans 12 makes clear.

Visually, the two phrases might be formatted to look something like

---

Active Spirituality   187

this: *DISCERNMENT of the will of God* (Catholic), emphasizing the process; *Discernment of THE WILL OF GOD* (Protestant), emphasizing the goal. Quaker tradition seeks to integrate the two, where the task of the Christian life is seen as continual discernment, emphasizing community.

Discernment Revisited: An Ignatian Process

The process of discernment developed by Ignatius of Loyola offers a creative blend of mind and heart, drawing on cognitive and affective prayer experiences. This is *not* a prayer exercise that you simply sit down and "do" but rather one that will continue over several months. Because it is part of Ignatius' *Spiritual Exercises* based on the life of Christ, it should be used in conjunction with daily praying with scripture, with a series of meetings to reflect with a spiritual guide.

The Ignatian model is congruent with and enriched by the communal emphasis of Reformed, Wesleyan, and Quaker perspectives.

PRAYER EXERCISE 42: An Ignatian Discernment Process

There are three occasions for making a good choice: (1) When the will is moved to know without hesitation; (2) when much light is received through desolations and consolations—up one day, down the next; (3) when, in a time of tranquillity, one feels no strong pull either way.

As you face some potential change in your life:
● *Gather information* from sources such as your experience, scripture, the community, reading, counseling, or interviewing.
● *State the proposed change in positive form:* I will make this change. . . .
● *Place the choice before "the mind's eye,"* and imagine how you will feel if you make the change. This helps to avoid "emotional jet-lag," that is, making a decision and discovering too late how it will affect your emotions. When considering a new job, picture

yourself at the desk in the new office, in the pulpit of that church, in the kitchen or factory where you would work.

● *Offer those images to God,* using a releasing litany such as the Jesus Prayer, and develop an *attitude of* indifference, praying that you make the decision for the greater glory of God. Cultivate this attitude of neutrality by following the pattern of Christ: "Your will be done." Upon every recollection of a potential choice—opening a letter, talking with another person, getting a phone call—use some releasing litany.

● *Weigh the "pros and cons,"* not the same as counting them! You may have only two "cons," but if one involves breaking off all relationships with children and spouse, that single "con" may *weigh* more than five "pros." After weighing, which is more reasonable?

● *Finally, offer the decision to God* and await an inner confirmation; or go through the process of "desolations and consolations" again (point 2, above), continuing the process until there is a sense of peace.

● Other questions: What would you say to *a colleague in a similar situation?* Picture yourself *on your deathbed:* What choice would you wish you had made? *Before Christ your Judge and Beloved,* what choice would you wish you had made?

● Thumb-nail sketch: How does this decision sit with your *head?* Your *heart?* Your *faith journey?* Test it with past experience.

Discernment Revisited: A Re-formed Perspective

Calvin drew on the Orthodox idea of the "energies of God." Basil of Caesarea, living in the fourth century before the East-West and Reformation splits, wrote: "We know our God from [divine] energies, but we do not claim that we can draw near to [divine] essence (*ousia*). For [divine] energies come down to us, but [the divine] essence remains unapproachable."

Following Basil, Calvin said we can never know God in Godself (Latin *a se*) but *only God as God interacts* with us as creatures. Philosopher-mathematician Alfred North Whitehead expressed this distinction as "the primordial nature of God" (essence) and the "consequent nature of God" (energies). Trying to know the "divine essence" is "mere speculation" for Calvin, and the way to avoid such speculation is *to pray, the chief "exercise" of faith!*

☐ The concept of the "energies of God" becomes an extremely practical metaphor to understand how it is that by touching "the least of these," *we are touched by God in the hidden Messiah.* It is the Emmanuel model, the secret presence God. So we are energized not only by our inner joy, but also by our experiences of the world's need: Nature is "the theater of God's glory" (Calvin), and divine energies radiate through the beauty and even the violence of creation and the least of its creatures.

☐ Focusing on divine "energies" rather than "essence" leads *from passive speculation to active discernment:* How is God calling me *now?* Following the pattern of Mark's gospel as Jesus moves from place to place *immediately,* our vocational discernment is urgent: Compassion flows from how you act right now; future intentions don't count.[2] Paradoxically, what you do is only one tiny "act" or "scene" in the eternal "theater" of God's glory: "Do your work as if you had a thousand years to live, and as if you were to die tomorrow," said Mother Ann of the Shakers.

☐ To focus on the energies of God as the source for discerning God's will leads us to be attentive to the sources of our own vocational energies, primarily from two sources: your own deep gladness and the world's deep hunger.[3] At times we are energized more by one than the other, but where the two meet there can be virtual electricity! In Robert Frost's words:

> But yield who will to their separation,
> My object in life is to unite
> My vocation and my avocation
> As my two eyes make one in sight.
> Only where love and need are one,
> And the work is play for mortal stakes,
> Is the deed ever really done
> For heaven and the future's sakes.[4]

Conversely, lack of energy may be a call to explore your unique inward delight or a call to some outward need.

Vocation includes these two: an *inner* sense of call (your deep gladness, discerned through solitude) and an *outer* verification of that call (the world's deep hunger, discerned through service). But there is a third element, *an affirmation by the "church"* (discerned through community). Discernment as *shema* means attentive listening to God through all three.

Most churches have some process like this in place for clergy, but few offer any parallel for laypeople. Yet discerning one's vocation is not merely private: It is an "ecclesiastical" matter, a concern of the community. *Klesis* (calling) is the root for *ekklesia* (church), literally "the called out ones." (See "Creating a Vocational Support Group," on page 193) But discerning your *mission* is a prerequisite for choosing or changing *career*.

PRAYER EXERCISE 43: My Life Mission Statement

> **I think it would be well, and proper, and obedient, and pure, to grasp your one necessity and not let it go, to dangle from it limp wherever it takes you. Then even death, where you're going no matter how you live, cannot you part.**
> **—Annie Dillard, *Teaching a Stone to Talk***

What is my purpose for being on this earth? "If the eye is *single*, your whole body will be full of light" (Matthew 6:22).[5] What is the *intent* behind the *content* of your serving? The first part of your mission you share with all humanity: to stay in the Presence, to *be* before you *do*: "Seek the Missioner before the mission," then in gratitude for your life make the world a better place.[6] The second part of your mission, unique to you, embraces both themes in the unique context of *your* life:

● Some deep gladness within you: *What puts a sparkle in your eyes?*

● Some deep hunger of the world: *What pulls at your heartstrings?*

Put *your* flesh on *your* mission, but draft it paradoxically between being too general or too specific: You might say "to lay
bricks," but what if you couldn't use your hands? You might say
"to glorify God" or "help others," then add "through" or "by . . . "
Example: "To express the joy in my life through the arts, cutting
across cultures, especially with children." Let it speak to working
years or retirement; if you should be disabled or held hostage. Your
"why to live" can sustain you through many outer *career* changes.
Rework your statement. Repeat it to yourself as a "prayer," your
heart's deepest yearning. Put it on a card inside your closet door or
your desk or in your wallet.

Discernment Revisited: A Wesleyan Perspective

This adaptation of the so-called "Wesleyan quadrilateral" provides a
balanced discerning process. Wesley drew on scripture (as the primary
source of guidance) yet also on the community, past as well as present,
reason and experience:

scripture

tradition   reason

experience

Drawing on the Reformers and Ignatius, Wesley gave priority to
scripture. Whenever Calvin questioned the proper interpretation of a
particular scripture, he would turn first to the earliest church fathers and
mothers, then to Augustine, and successively to later interpretations.

So part of "gathering the information" in discerning God's will is to
ask what Christians in other times and places have said about a particular
issue (*tradition*); to use the best research to analyze their conclusions
(*reason*); and then offer the issue to God in light of your *experience*,
which for Wesley meant *spiritual experience*, surrendering to God by
"testing one's leadings." Here is where traditional churches let us down:
The Quaker communal discernment process is a laboratory for Wesley's
experiential dimension.

Discernment Revisited: Communal Model of the Friends

Originally developed by the Friends for discernment when two people want to be married, "the clearness committee" is adapted now for people facing a variety of "vocational" struggles. It is a method that seekers and ministers might offer to friends trying to discern what is best.

PRAYER EXERCISE 44: The Clearness Committee

The person seeking clearness writes his or her situation in advance and circulates it to five or six trusted persons whom he or she invites. The meeting begins with centering prayer and silence. Then the "focus person" gives a fresh statement of the concern. This is followed by discerning questions (Have you considered . . . ?), but not "fix-it" advice (Why don't you. . . ?) Then some observations: I'm hearing four possible careers. . . . All is in a prayerful atmosphere. The session may end with "the laying on of hands" in prayer. The group may be reconvened.[7]

Creating a Vocational Support Group

Using all these—the Ignatian "process" of discernment, Reformed and Quaker emphasis on community, and Wesleyan emphasis on sources of light—local churches can "continue the incarnation" by developing support groups for vocational discernment. Occasionally, meetings might explore Bolles's *What Color Is Your Parachute?*, the Ignatian process, or these chapters. But the main purpose of the group should be to *network and pray* for one another.

I recently attended Trinity Episcopal Church in Princeton, New Jersey, and in the literature rack I saw a pamphlet, *JobSeekers*. While it is primarily oriented around career, it also includes broader issues of vocation. Issues range from short-term mission service to long-term career changes. Attendees range in age from just-out-of-school to senior citizens. For ten years the church has been providing a continuing "clearness committee" for people trying to connect their gifts with some hunger of the world, testing their personal leadings with the leadings of the Spirit through the group.

The discipline of community ought to mean that we help one another with our mundane yet sometimes life-and-death decisions. The base communities in Latin America interweave Bible study, problem sharing, community action, and prayer with discernment in a communal context.

A church-related vocational support group involves all five spiritual disciplines: the discipline of *solitude* (prayerful attentiveness to your own giftedness), the discipline of *heart and mind* (research in your field, career counseling outside the group, and spiritual study), the discipline of *service* (your previous work experiences), and the discipline of *community* (the support group itself). All these help a person discern what is called for in one's present context: *the discipline* of *vocation.*

The Trinity of Experience: The "Art" of Discernment

Some people, more than others, are tantalized with vocational fantasies of what might have been or might still be. You picture yourself as the chief executive of a company or president of the labor union; as a star musician, actor, politician, or author; as having children if you have none; as being married if you are single or single if you are married; as living out your sexual orientation with a different partner or by being celibate; as being a physician if you are a teacher; as being a mission worker in the Third World if you live in the USA.

Vocational fantasies may be distractions, temptations to leave one's deep center in Christ, or they may reflect deeper genuine stirrings of the Spirit. Some choices more than others are "moral issues" of commitment, but we need to remember that even things that are *good in themselves,* such as "bread" in the story of Jesus' temptations, can take us wildly off course! "But test everything; hold fast to what is good" (I Thessalonians 5:21).

I have titled this section "The Trinity of Experience" because there are three options for dealing as Christians with unrestful vocational fantasies.

1. *Movement away,* experienced as *negation (kenosis).* More likely

than not, even if later we are invited to move toward a particular "beckoning," first we need the discipline to wrestle with it, fight it, and try to empty it. It is the guidance I was given by an older pastor: "Don't be a minister if you can possibly avoid it!" Other professionals give similar advice. We need to wrestle with the discipline of the heart and mind: Is there any clear teaching in scripture or the Christian community that would oppose our acting on our dreams? Or is it a matter of discerning what is "best" (Philippians 1:10) among equally valid options?

There are times when a "vocation of emptiness" is given to us. One may go through a long discernment process before reaching the point of embracing this "apophatic way." You may live never having children, never becoming a minister or a musician, or never committing to a sexual relationship. But by having directly entertained such a possibility, you can now embrace the emptiness and offer it as "space for God"—and your life will be infinitely richer.

2. *Movement toward*, experienced as *fulfillment* (*pleroma*). If you are convinced that there is no clear guidance from scripture and the Christian community that would preclude a course of action, after "praying" by gathering the data, weighing the pros and cons, and doing the other steps of the discernment process, then offer the decision to God. Test it with your past experiences and with the community. If you still feel called, it is time to take the leap of faith. A young adult sets out for foreign service; a minister in his thirties goes to medical school; a political science professor goes to seminary; a single woman adopts a child. It is the "kataphatic way" of embracing the invitation.

And sometimes we know only by embracing the opportunity and being emptied through it that we must return to embrace the emptiness again. But God can use even our deceits, false starts as well as false hopes, *if we surrender them* as they happen to us along the way. Other times, we are called to yet a third way.

3. *Dance, movement back and forth*, experienced as *both/and* (*paradoxa*). It is the "way of creative integration." Sometimes we are being invited to be "in the world, yet not of the world" and to live that way in relation to some vocational quest, as in the business executive who is also a poet or musician; the mechanic who always wanted to be a pastor, but now *ministers* as the beloved youth advisor.

This is not an easy way: If you fail to go through the emptying process, the fantasies become addictive. The way to genuine vocational integration is through the *cross* and *resurrection*. Only if you contemplate and empty life's choices do they come back as genuine gifts to meet a real hunger. Schweitzer gave up being a theologian to become a missionary and physician but ended up being all those, plus musician and mystic! Quaker artist Edward Hicks earned a living as a commercial sign painter, but expressed his deepest joy in dozens of versions of *The Peaceable Kingdom,* uniting the vision of Isaiah 11:6-9 with the Quaker dream of peace in the "new world."

The apophatic way *away from* the world (the cross) and the kataphatic way *toward* the world (resurrection) can lead to a unitive third way, *paradoxically* transforming the world (Pentecost). There are times in our lives when we are emptied, other times when we are filled, still other times when we dance with a rhythm of the two experiences in our lives.

• The creative process of an artist, adapted from Dorothy Sayers, provides a practical analogy of the trinity of spiritual experience.[8] First, there is *the creative idea,* born out of emptiness: "The earth was without form and void." Then comes the creative expression as the word becomes flesh–incarnation: Clay is molded; stone is sculptured; words are written on a page; paint is splashed on the canvas; notes are penned on the music score. Finally, the idea and its expression are unified as *creative synergy,* "creative interpretation" takes what was done in time and makes it timeless. Mozart's music is performed and my spine tingles; I see the *Mona Lisa* and feel liberated; I read *Les Miserables* and Jean Valjean creates compassion in me. This is the Spirit—Jesus who lived becomes the living Christ.

• Every Christian is a unique artist. And this is the pattern for returning to your "original" state of art: Continually empty the self to allow the creative Word of love to be enfleshed in you, *expressed through your life's mission so that the world may interpret,* "may see and believe."

Dancing with the Disciplines: Living Off Balance

Our vocation is be attentive to the dynamic balance of *bearing fruits* in the world and returning to our *spiritual roots.* "I pray that . . . you may be strengthened in your inner being with power through [God's] Spirit, and that Christ may dwell in your hearts through faith, as you are being *rooted and grounded in love*" (Ephesians 3:16-17, italics added).

The words *dance* and *discipline* do not seem to go together. Yet they represent the paschal mystery of *joy* and *sacrifice,* as Richard Foster captured in his book title *The Celebration of Discipline.* So dance with the disciplines! "Jesus thrown everything off balance," says the Misfit in a Flannery O'Connor story. Life is not always neatly balanced; the roots and the tree are not always symmetrical. The goal of spiritual disciplines is not so much an equilibrium as *learning to live off balance!*

Life becomes a dance between activity and sabbath, woundings on the edge and renewings at the center, until in a momentary turning to God out on the edge, the circle envelops you again. You are back home while still on the journey. All life, not just worship, is a celebration! "God is a circle whose center is everywhere / And whose circumference is nowhere," wrote Meister Eckhart. Back and forth it goes until the moving rim and the still point are one. At every turn, you meet God.

Vocation as a lifelong discernment process is the beginning *and* the end of the spiritual life: "I beseech you that ye walk worthy of the vocation wherewith ye have been called" (Ephesians 4:1 KJV). We cannot find our true calling, our "walk" in life, without stumbling on the way. Through our "graced stumblings" in each of these disciplines—being with others, or being alone, reflecting with the mind and heart, testing our wings in service—we discern our vocation: *God, how are you inviting me now?*

Vocation is spirituality for a purpose: to discern God's design for my being on this earth, to surrender the pain *and* joy of my finite life as a part of the infinite Mystery of Christ at work re-birthing the world. *It is never too late:* Like Joseph and his family in Egypt, one moment of "revelation" can give meaning to years of futility, just as one moment of sexual bliss can give birth to a whole new life! *Trust God in this very moment, redeeming those very moments.*

Most of you reading this will be discerning your *being* in Christ in the midst of your *doing* in the world—dancing with the disciplines—being emptied and being filled. So I offer this as my prayer that your deep gladness will find a place where it meets a deep hunger of the world:

> *Master:* As a tree dies cut off from its roots, so you will die in the midst of worldly business. To live you need to return to your roots.
> *Disciple:* Should I leave my business and go into a monastery?
> *Master:* By no means! The roots need the branches to give life. Stay in the world and return to your heart.

If you re-turn to the deepest yearning of your heart, you will not be able for long to avoid the yearning of the world—and of the One who is the resilient Mystery at the heart of existence.

To yearn is to pray.

Let us pray.

Goals for Spiritual Disciplines

A Self-Assessment for Personal Growth and Congregational Renewal

God's love expressed in Jesus Christ is a free gift of grace: Like a loving parent waiting to welcome a child home, God longs to embrace us as we respond in faith, hope, and love. As we return home to God, we need training for the spiritual journey to rekindle the flame of faith and continually reflect the love of Christ. The following goals represent basic disciplines from the Bible based on the pattern of Christ's life and the lives of "saints" of the church. They are like five spokes in a wheel connecting our outward activity with the still center of sabbath rest and renewal, all surrounded by *prayer and scripture* that form the rim.

The Discipline of Community. Corporate worship is the vital nerve that nurtures the muscles of our faith. Believers surrender to God and care for each other, opening ourselves to God's call to learn and serve. Following the pattern of Christ's early disciples, other expressions of community include one-on-one spiritual friendship (formally or informally), families, and small groups for support, study, or service in the church or larger community (Hebrews 12:25; Psalm 122:1; Romans 12; 1 Corinthians 11:23-26; 12:1-27; 13:1-13).

The Discipline of Solitude. The psalm writers and spiritual mentors reflect the rhythm of Jesus' life, serving in community and retreating in solitude for prayer. A daily quiet time for personal prayer and scripture meditation, with occasional longer retreat times, has always been an important source of guidance and strength for Christians. From Quaker and Catholic contemplative traditions, from Calvin, Luther and Wesley, from Albert Schweitzer, Martin Luther King, Jr., and Mother Teresa, we know that the life of action requires the life of prayer: You cannot pour water from an empty cup (Psalm 46:10; 1 Thessalonians 5:16-18; Mark 1:35-37; 6:30-46).

The Discipline of Heart and Mind. Every Christian is a *disciple*—the root of the word *discipline*—called to a commitment to life-long learning from Christ the Master Teacher: "Take my yoke upon you and learn from me." Church leaders and members, adults and children, set an example: By pursuing personal reading, classes, and telling stories of faith, the character is formed to reflect God's love in our homes and places of influence (Matthew 11:28-30; 28:16-20; 2 Peter 3:18; Acts 2:42).

The Discipline of Service. Stewardship is responding to God's "first love" for us by "giving back." The Good Samaritan provides the twofold pattern: (1) direct, one-on-one service and (2) indirect service by support of helping institutions. Worship is service and service becomes prayer: We intercede by yearning for others in our hearts before God and in our actions by advocating on their behalf. Throughout the Old and New Covenant *tithing* has been a model of systematic, proportionate giving of our resources of time, talent, and treasure (Galatians 6:2; 2 Corinthians 9:6-15; Malachi 3:10; Hebrews 7:3-8; Mark 10:40-45; Romans 12).

The Discipline of Vocation. Our "calling" is to contemplate God's deep love—and to discern how to manifest that love in the world: "The place God calls you to is the place where your deep gladness and the world's deep hunger meet."* Vocation is a lifelong process of discernment, alone and with others: What is my purpose in life? How can successes *and* problems be used for good in each new situation? (Genesis 50:15-20; Romans 12:1-3; 8:28; Ephesians 4:1-7; John 15:1-5; Galatians 5:22-23; Philippians 1:9-11; *Frederick Buechner).

Personal Growth
Prayerfully assess your own spiritual life in light of a desire for a balanced Christian life. Note for yourself at least one discipline where you are making a re-commitment, praying for specific ways to be renewed in that area. (Idea: Give the note to a friend to return to you in six months.) If you want to grow in service, you might jot down specific ways of serving that occur to you; to grow in community, you might choose to find a "spiritual companion" or become part of a support group or increase participation in worship or communion; if you want to deepen your solitude, you might make a commitment to set aside specific time for daily prayer, and to attend a spiritual retreat.

Congregational Renewal
The above disciplines might first be introduced first to church officers, asking for personal commitment and official action by the board to give a printed copy to all existing leaders and members and prospective members. For this to take on personal meaning and commitment, the disciplines could be introduced in the format of a spiritual retreat using exercises from this book. Then something like the statement below could be printed and circulated along with the five disciplines.

● *Example*: [The pastoral and lay leadership of the congregation are committed to these five spiritual disciplines as goals for deepening our discipleship. We hope that all who lead—committee members, teachers, advisors, choirs—as well as long-term and new members of the church will also make their commitment to these goals.]

● *Another Option:* The board might also assess the balance of the congregation's own corporate life in relation to the five disciplines, any need to increase its communal emphasis in one or more of these areas, and specific ways of prayer and action to do it. This could also be done in a retreat setting or could involve the congregation in small group meetings with church members.

From Committee to Community

A Model for Creating Intentional Community in Ordinary Meetings

Purpose

To enable "the meeting of persons" in ordinary meetings, in the local church and at regional levels. It need take only six to fifteen minutes of the meeting and can facilitate the agenda and improve the decision making!

● Start using this process with the pastoral staff and boards as they set the tone for the entire church. Large churches need this to keep them caring: First Presbyterian Church, Bethlehem, Pennsylvania—with more than 3,000 members—has been using an approach like this for decades. Small and average-sized churches need not fear that growth will make them less personal as long as they provide safe places for sharing.

● The paschal mystery of the crucified-risen Christ sets the pattern: Blessing comes out of sharing the brokenness of the world or our lives. "Rejoice with those who rejoice, weep with those who weep" (Romans 12:15).

Process

Step 1. Pair off one-on-one, suggesting persons meet with "someone you know the least," and use any questions that promote genuine sharing: What is some *joy* that I have experienced since we last met? What is some *concern* on my heart right now? (Allow five minutes, two or three minutes per person. Leader give a signal at half-way point and again at the end by clapping the hands one time or ringing a soft bell).

Step 2. Leader: Suggest that each pair spend one minute in *silent prayer*, closing eyes and picturing the face of the partner, lifting up that person's joy with thanksgiving and silently praying for the concern. Then give the partner some sign of Christ's peace. *Other options*: Offer a "sentence prayer" for each other, still in pairs, or with group as a whole (see variations, below).

Step 3. Conclude by singing a verse of a hymn or a spiritual. Examples: "Spirit of the Living God" or "Kum Ba Yah." The variations for building koinonia are endless. Use your creativity and humor to create community!

Variations on Sharing

Variations on time and numbers: If you have a time limit of six to fifteen minutes, then one-on-one sharing works best so that each person has enough "air time" to share significantly. It is also easier for some to open up to just *one* other person. If it is a fellowship meeting (youth, men, women) where time is not a problem, you might have groups as large as seven.

A scripture text can be used as the basis for the sharing; *The Serendipity Bible* or any books by Lyman Coleman may be adapted. For example, recalling the story of the Good Samaritan, the leader might then ask people to share *an experience of a time since the group last met when you have observed* (in your church, family, community, or anywhere in the world!): (a) an example of a person in need (the wounded person), (b) an example of a person who gave some direct help (a "Samaritan"), or (c) an example of indirect helping through a helping institution— "paying the innkeeper" to continue the compassion. Then conclude with prayers, step 2 above, or any variations, below.

Variations on Prayer

After completing steps 1 and 2, you might convene *the group as a whole* and announce there will be a silent time during your prayers of thanksgiving for those who are comfortable to mention *thanksgivings* in a word or phrase; then after a brief prayer of petition, there will be a time to mention *concerns* briefly—*using just a name, place, and brief description of the concern:* Example: " . . . for Ruth in San Francisco, who is in the hospital with cancer." Then the leader may offer a prayer, or the group may sing a hymn as a prayer.

Another Variation—A "Quaker Meeting"

Here is a brief, *modified form of a Friends Meeting:* Use one or two daily lectionary reading(s) or other scripture(s) you choose; you might use a brief order for "evening prayer." Announce that there will be *silence for prayer and reflection* (eyes closed or open) for five minutes after the reading of _____, and that during that time one or at most three persons may offer some brief words of reflection. *Emphasize that it is all right if no one speaks, and that the silence is time to reflect on the scripture, to pray for the meeting and its members.*

Another Variation—An "Emmaus Walk"

In this ancient practice, two people walk together for five or ten minutes, as in the "Walk to Emmaus" in Luke 24:13-35. (You need not read the entire passage; just summarize the highlights.) The exercise is excellent in good weather but can also be done indoors with people walking to some spot in the building to sit and converse. It may be used with the questions in step 1, above. After reconvening at a given time, a song may serve as a group prayer, or say the Lord's Prayer.

Other Resources

See Roberta Hestenes, *Turning Committees into Communities* (NavPress, 1991); and also by Hestenes, "Building Christian Community through Small Groups," an audio-cassette package (Fuller Theological Seminary Media Services Dept.). Also see Philip Anderson, *Church Meetings That Matter* (New York: The Pilgrim Press, 1987).

NOTES

Introduction

1. Carlo Carretto, *The God Who Comes* (London: Darton, Longman and Todd, 1981), quoted in *A Guide to Prayer for Ministers and Other Servants* (Nashville: The Upper Room, 1983), 74.

2. A few basic books on spirituality: Richard Foster, *The Celebration of Discipline*, rev. ed. (San Francisco: Harper & Row, 1988); Alan Jones, *Journey into Christ* (Cambridge, Mass.: Cowley, 1992); Howard Rice, *Reformed Spirituality: An Introduction for Believers* (Louisville: Westminster/John Knox Press, 1991); Anthony DeMello, *Sadhana: A Way to God: Christian Exercises in Eastern Form* (Garden City, N.Y.: Doubleday, Image, 1978); Tilden Edwards, *Living in the Presence: Disciplines for the Spiritual Heart* (San Francisco: Harper & Row, 1987); M. Scott Peck, *The Road Less Traveled* (New York: Simon & Schuster, 1980); Kenneth Leech, *Soul Friend* (San Francisco: Harper & Row, 1977); and *any* book by Henri Nouwen, especially *The Wounded Healer* (Garden City, N.Y.: Doubleday, Image, 1979); *With Open Hands* (Notre Dame, Ind.: Ave Maria Press, 1972).

3. The words "I am the way" convey a sense of a continuing pilgrimage, so I have translated the Greek *hodos* as "journey" in John 14:6. Also when Luke refers to the Christian religion as "the Way" (Acts 9:2; 19:23; 22:4) it is not just as "a point of entry" to God, but as a continuing "Emmaus journey" (Luke 24:13-35) where the risen Christ accompanies believers on their pilgrimage.

Chapter 1

1. See Jacques Ellul, *What I Believe* (Grand Rapids: Eerdmans, 1989), 148.

2. See Acts 10:4, 30, 34-35. The Gentile Cornelius had been praying, then Peter realizes that God shows no favoritism but hears the prayers of all.

3. John Berger, "You Can't God Home: The Hidden Pain of 20th Century Life," *Utne Reader* (May-June 1990): 85-87.

4. There is always debate as to whether the Good Samaritan story is merely an ethical imperative for us to love our neighbor, or whether Luke also is making a spiritual-theological point about our spiritual bankruptcy. I believe that Luke purposely combines the two. It is impossible to love my neighbor genuinely unless I have put myself in the other's place. The surprise of grace is that I cannot truly love a neighbor until I recognize that I am a broken "Samaritan"! Christ consistently comes in the disguise of the poor and rejected and the stranger (Matthew 25:31-46; Luke 24:13-35). What seems like a simple command to do good moves to a deeper spiritual level of confronting me with my own need for God.

5. Diogenes Allen gives us a helpful summary of these in a very readable book, *Three Outsiders: Pascal, Kierkegaard, and Simone Weil* (Cambridge, Mass.: Cowley, 1983).

Chapter 2

1. Paul Tillich, "You Are Accepted," in *The Shaking of the Foundations* (New York: Scribner's, 1948), 155.

2. Somerset Maugham, *Of Human Bondage* (New York: Doubleday, 1936), 106, continues: "But the young know they are wretched, . . . full of the truthless ideals which have been instilled into them, and each time they come in contact with the real they are bruised and wounded." Daniel Levinson, et al., write in *The Seasons of a Man's Life* (New York: Alfred A. Knopf, 1978) that no man can get to age forty without some experience of human destructiveness; Gail Sheehy in *Passages* (New

York: Bantam Books, 1977) says much the same for men and women; Carl Jung wrote in *Modern Man in Search of a Soul* (New York: Harcourt Brace Jovanovich, Harvest) that by age thirty-five to forty, every crisis was basically a religious one.

3. See Gerald G. May, M.D., *Addiction and Grace* (San Francisco: Harper & Row, 1988) for an excellent treatment of the relation of our psychological addictions to the spiritual life.

4. John Cheever, *The Stories of John Cheever* (New York: Alfred E. Knopf, 1978), 459-60.

5. See Henri J. M. Nouwen, *The Wounded Healer* (Garden City, N.Y.: Doubleday, Image, 1979), 84.

6. There is a parallel of these two ideas in Christina Grof's work, "Addiction as Spiritual Emergency" (cassettes produced by Sounds True Recordings, 1825 Pearl St., Boulder, CO 80302). By *spiritual emergency* she refers to a crisis in one's experience of addiction leading to a new life-orientation, while the term *spiritual emergence* refers to a more gradual change.

7. See 2 Timothy 1:5; 3:15.

8. Herman Hesse, *Siddartha*, trans. Hilda Rosner (New York: New Directions, 1957). Hesse, of German background growing up in India, highlights common themes of Eastern religions and Western Christianity in the saga of a youth moving into middle and then older years. Siddartha first follows the worldly path and then after a series of "disillusionments" begins to dis-cover what is Real.

9. For an excellent discussion of these paradoxically divergent paths of becoming and being a Christian, see Charles Williams, *The Descent of the Dove* (Grand Rapids: Eerdmans, 1939), chaps. 1-2.

10. Throughout this manuscript, I have substituted "Child of Humanity" for "Son of Man" in the New Revised Standard Version; see "Mime" in chapter 15.

11. A rich phrase from Simone Weil, *Waiting for God,* trans. Emma Craufurd (New York: Putnam, 1951).

12. The Bible speaks of salvation as past, "in hope we were saved" (Romans 8:24); present, "to us who are being saved" (1 Corinthians 1:18); and future, "Much more . . . will we be saved through [Christ]" (Romans 5:8). This ongoing process of salvation is our "sanctification,"

especially emphasized in Wesleyan tradition, becoming *holy* and *whole* (Leviticus 19:2; 1 Corinthians 1:2; 6:11; see part 2, theme 3, "The Discipline of Community").

13. *Space for God* is the title of an excellent book for personal or group study and prayer, by Don Postema (Grand Rapids: CRC, 1983).

14. T. S. Eliot, "Little Gidding," in *Four Quartets* (New York: Harcourt Brace Jovanovich, Harvest, 1971), 59.

Chapter 3

1. Soren Kierkegaard, *Fear and Trembling and Sickness unto Death,* trans. Walter Lowrie (Princeton, N.J.: Princeton University Press, 1968), 211.

2. Anne Morrow Lindberg, *Gift from the Sea* (New York: Random House, Vintage, 1955), 88; italics added.

3. See Charles Williams, *Descent of the Dove* (Grand Rapids: Eerdmans, 1939). I am indebted to Harry Skilton for first sharing this insight in an unpublished paper presented to Carlisle (Pa.) Presbytery Cleric, April 1986.

4. Matthew Fox, *Original Blessing* (Santa Fe: Bear, 1983), attributes four ways to Eckhart: *Via negativa, positiva, creativa,* and *transformativa.* But in the New Testament, "the transformative way" *includes* "the creative way." To be transformed is to be re-created in the image of God, to become re-generative partners with God's transformation of all nature (2 Corinthians 5:17; Romans 8:18-28; 12:1-3).

5. See "Revelation," in *Flannery O'Connor: The Complete Stories* (New York: Farrar, Straus & Giroux, 1988), 488-509.

Chapter 4

1. Alphonse and Rachel Goettmann, *Prayer of Jesus: Prayer of the Heart* (Mahwah, N.J.: Paulist Press, 1991), 59.

2. R. D. Laing, *The Politics of Experience* (New York: Ballantine, 1967), 44.

3. Frederick Buechner, *The Sacred Journey,* large print ed. (New York: Walker, 1982), 83.

4. Quoted in Diogenes Allen, *Three Outsiders: Pascal, Kierkegaard, and Simone Weil* (Cambridge, Mass.: Cowley, 1983), 73.

5. John Mulder and Hugh T. Kerr, eds., *Conversions* (Philadelphia: Westminster Press, 1983), give fifty brief biographies and writings of spiritual leaders from first century to the twentieth.

6. See Allen, *Three Outsiders*, 79.

7. Alan Paton, "Meditation for a Young Boy Being Confirmed," *The Christian Century*, 13 October 1954.

Chapter 5

1. Quoted in John Yungblut, *The Gentle Art of Spiritual Guidance* (Rockport, Mass.: Element, 1988), 84.

2. See R. D. Laing, *The Politics of Experience* (New York: Ballantine, 1967), 44.

3. Alex Haley, *Roots: The Saga of an American Family* (Garden City, N.Y.: Doubleday, 1976), 134.

4. Barry and Ann Ulinov, *Primary Speech* (Atlanta: John Knox Press, 1982), 105.

5. See R. D. Laing, *The Politics of Experience*, 44: "Wherever and whenever such a whorl of pattern sound or space is established in the external world, the power that it contains generates new lines of force whose effects are felt for centuries."

6. See Martha Welch, M.D., *Holding Time* (New York: Simon & Schuster, 1988).

7. Bernard Lafayette, Jr., director of the Martin Luther King, Jr., Center for Nonviolence, at Chautauqua Institution (N.Y.), July 1991.

8. See Eugene Peterson, *A Long Obedience in the Same Direction* (Downers Grove, Ill.: InterVarsity Press, 1989), 9-10.

Chapter 6

1. Carl Rogers, *On Becoming a Person* (Boston: Houghton Mifflin, 1961), 26.

2. Quoted in Matthew Fox, *Original Blessing: A Primer on Creation Spirituality* (Santa Fe: Bear, 1983), 92.

3. Brian Wren, "God Is One, Unique and Holy," in *The Presbyterian Hymnal* (Louisville: Westminster/John Knox Press, 1990), 135. Copyright by Hope Publishing Company, Carol Stream, IL 60188. International copyright secured. All rights reserved. Used by permission.

4. See Roberta Hestenes, *Turning Committees into Communities* (Colorado Springs: NavPress, 1991); and Roberta Hestenes, "Building Christian Community through Small Groups (Fuller Theological Seminary Media Services Dept.), an audio-cassette package. See also Lyman Coleman, *The Serendipity Bible for Groups* (Grand Rapids: Zondervan, 1986) and other books for small groups. Richard C. Meyer, *One Anothering: Biblical Building Blocks for Small Groups* (San Diego: LuriaMedia, 1990), outlines creative options for small groups.

5. Flannery O'Connor, *Mystery and Manners*, ed. Sally and Robert Fitzgerald (New York: Farrar, Straus & Giroux, 1969), 101. See also Flannery O'Connor, *The Habit of Being*, ed. Sally Fitzgerald (New York: Farrar, Straus & Giroux, 1979), xvii.

6. The theme is developed by Barry and Ann Ulinov, *Primary Speech* (Atlanta: John Knox Press, 1982).

7. See Lucian Richard, S.J., *The Spirituality of John Calvin* (Richmond: John Knox Press, 1978).

8. O'Connor, *The Habit of Being*, 517.

9. Quoted in Fox, *Original Blessing*, 266.

10. Suzanne Langer, *Philosophy in a New Key* (Cambridge, Mass.: Harvard University Press, 1957), offers the rich phrase, Music provides "a morophology of human senses."

11. T. S. Eliot, "The Dry Salvages," in *Four Quartets* (New York: Harcourt Brace Jovanovich, Harvest, 1971), 44.

12. Fred Pratt Green, "When In Our Music God Is Glorified," *The Presbyterian Hymnal*, 264. Copyright by Hope Publishing Company, Carol Stream, IL 60188. International copyright secured. All rights reserved. Used by permission.

Chapter 7

1. Thomas N. Hart, *The Art of Christian Listening* (Mahwah, N.J.: Paulist Press, 1980).

2. Dietrich Bonhoeffer, *Life Together* (New York: Harper & Row, 1954), 96.

3. The following books on spiritual direction are especially helpful: Alan Jones, *Exploring Spiritual Direction: An Essay on Christian Friendship* (New York: Seabury Press, 1982); Tilden Edwards, *Spiritual Friend: Reclaiming the Gift of Spiritual Direction* (Mahwah, N.J.: Paulist Press, 1980); William A. Barry and William J. Connolly, *The Practice of Spiritual Direction* (San Francisco: Harper & Row, 1982); Eugene Peterson, *Working the Angles* (Grand Rapids: Eerdmans, 1987); and Margaret Guenther, *Holy Listening* (Boston, MA: Cowley, 1992).

4. See Dietrich Bonhoeffer, *Letters and Papers from Prison*, trans. Eberhard Bethge (New York: Macmillan, 1971).

5. Robert Boyer, *Finding God at Home: Family Life as Spiritual Discipline* (San Francisco: Harper & Row, 1988).

6. See Philip Anderson, *Church Meetings That Matter* (New York: Pilgrim Press, 1987).

7. In Jewish tradition, the first five commands are related to loving God: Home (honoring parents) is the focus of honoring God and keeping sabbath The second five relate to loving neighbor.

8. Quoted in Bengt R. Hoffman, *Luther and the Mystics* (Minneapolis: Augsburg, 1976), 187, italics added.

9. In the Hebrew Bible, Deuteronomy 6:5-11 is referred to as a "little creed." In the New Testament there is a simple creed or confession, "Jesus Christ is Lord," within a longer creed (Philippians 2:5-11). Colossians 1:12-20 is another, both probably hymns as well as creeds, meant as "sung prayers." See also Romans 10:9 and I Corinthians 12:3.

10. Dietrich Bonhoeffer, *Life Together*, 77-78.

Chapter 8

1. Segundo Galilea, "Politics and Contemplation: The Mystical and Political Dimensions of the Christian Faith," in *The Mystical and Political Dimensions of the Christian Faith,* ed. Claude Geffre and Gustavo Gutierrz (New York: Herder & Herder, 1974), 28.

2. "The Word very near you; it is in your mouth and in your heart . . ." (Deuteronomy 30:14, see Romans 10:8).

3. Dietrich Bonhoeffer, *Meditating on the Word* (Nashville: The Upper Room, 1988), 29-30.

4. Dietrich Bonhoeffer, *Life Together* (New York: Harper & Row, 1954), 78-79.

5. T. S. Eliot, "Little Gidding," in *Four Quartets* (Harcourt, Brace, Jovanovich, 1968).

6. See Tilden Edwards, *Sabbath Time* (Nashville: The Upper Room, 1992) for creative personal, church, and family dimensions of sabbath.

7. See "A Good Man Is Hard to Find," in *Flannery O'Connor: The Complete Stories* (New York: Farrar, Straus & Giroux, 1988), 132.

Chapter 9

1. Simone Weil, *Waiting for God,* trans. Emma Craufurd (New York: Putnam, 1951), 120-21.

2. Francis Kelly Nemeck, OMI, and Marie Theresa Coombs, hermit, *O Blessed Night: Recovering from Addiction, Codependency, and Attachment based on Insights of St. John of the Cross and Pierre Teilhard de Chardin* (New York: Alba House, 1991), see especially chapter 8.

Chapter 10

1. R. A. Brown and R. G. Luckock, "Dreams, Daydreams and Discovery," in *Journal of Chemical Education* 55, no. 11 (November 1978).

2. A helpful book relates the MBTI to methods of prayer as well as offering practical prayer exercises: Chester P. Michael and Marie C. Norrisey, *Prayer and Temperament* (Charlottesville, Va.: The Open Door, 1984).

3. See M. Basil Pennington, *Centering Prayer* (Garden City, N.Y.: Doubleday, Image, 1980).

4. Both, published by The Upper Room (Nashville), include classical readings and prayers.

5. See John Mulder and Hugh T. Kerr, eds., *Conversions* (Philadelphia: Westminster Press, 1983). Fifty brief biographies adaptable to one's personal prayer time.

6. Ben Campbell Johnson, *To Will God's Will* (Atlanta: John Knox Press, 1987) includes an excellent section on "Journaling: An Important Tool for the Spiritual Journey."

7. See John Sanford, *Dreams: God's Forgotten Language* (New York: Harper & Row, 1989); and Morton Kelsey, *Dreams: A Way to Listen to God* (Mahwah, N.J.: Paulist Press, 1978).

8. Henri J. M. Nouwen, *Behold the Beauty of the Lord: Praying with Icons* (Notre Dame, Ind.: Ave Maria, 1987).

9. *The Way of a Pilgrim,* trans. R. M. French (San Francisco: HarperCollins) and other publishers.

10. Ben and Carol Weir with Dennis Benson, *Hostage Bound, Hostage Free* (Philadelphia: Westminster Press, 1987).

Chapter 11

1. For more on the relation of science and faith, see Thomas Torrance, *Christian Theology and Scientific Culture* (New York: Oxford University Press, 1981); and Diogenes Allen, *Christian Belief in a Post-Modern World* (Louisville: Westminster/John Knox Press, 1989).

2. Robert Coles, *Flannery O'Connor's South* (Baton Rouge: Louisiana State University Press, 1980), 159.

Chapter 12

1. Ashley Montagu, *Growing Young* (New York: McGraw-Hill, 1981), 117, italics added.

2. Andrew Purves, *The Search for Compassion: Spirituality in Ministry* (Philadelphia: Westminster Press, 1989).

3. Rainer Maria Rilke, *Letters to a Young Poet,* trans. M. D. Herter Norton (New York: W. W. Norton, 1954), 35.

4. See William Bausch, *Storytelling: Imagination and Faith* (Mystic, Conn.: Twenty-Third Publications, 1989); and Robert Coles, *The*

Call of Stories (Boston: Houghton Mifflin, 1989).

5. See Robert Ornstein and Richard F. Thompson, *The Amazing Brain* (Boston: Houghton Mifflin, 1986).

6. See John Mulder and Hugh Kerr, eds., *Conversions* (Philadelphia: Westminster, 1983), brief stories of great Christians.

7. See Anne Broyles, *Journaling: A Spirit Journey* (Nashville: The Upper Room, 1988).

8. Mary Oliver, *House of Light* (Boston: Beacon Press, 1990).

9. *In Generation to Generation: Family Process in Church and Synagogue* (New York: The Guilford Press, 1985), 157-159, Edwin Friedman tells how an anxious and angry Henry Marvin is forever changed because a minister paid attention to his own intuition, then reported a story with circumstances similar to Marvin's—jolting the man into seeing himself. See also Edwin Friedman, *Friedman's Fables* (New York: The Guilford Press, 1990).

10. Ornstein and Thompson, *The Amazing Brain*, 181-82.

Chapter 13

1. Albert Schweitzer, *The Quest of the Historical Jesus* (New York: Macmillan, 1968), 403, italics added.

2. For an excellent, fresh translation, see Thomas a Kempis, *The Imitation of Christ*, ed. William C. Creasey (Notre Dame, Ind.: Ave Maria Press, 1989).

3. M. Scott Peck, M.D., *The Different Drummer: Community Making and Peace* (New York: Simon & Schuster, 1987), 216-17.

4. Paraphrase of an ancient aphorism that was a favorite of Luther.

5. Nicholas Berdyaev, *The Divine and the Human* (London: Geoffrey Bles, 1949), 12.

Chapter 14

1. Ernest Boyer, Jr., *Finding God at Home: Family Life as Spiritual Discipline* (San Francisco: Harper & Row, 1988), 23.

2. Quoted in Perry D. LeFevre, *The Prayers of Kierkegaard* (Chicago: University of Chicago Press, 1963), 98.

Chapter 15

1. C. S. Lewis, *The Screwtape Letters* (London: Collins, Fontana, 1962), 46.

2. See Daniel 7:13-27 where "one like a son of man [child of humanity]" refers to "The suffering saints of the most high" (a phrase used four times), who eventually are vindicated in the presence of God.

3. Karl Barth, *Evangelical Theology: An Introduction*, trans. Grover Foley (New York: Holt, Rinehart and Winston, 1963), 136.

4. Dietrich Bonhoeffer, *Letters and Papers from Prison*, trans. Eberhard Bethge, paper ed. (New York: The Macmillan, 1972), 381-83, presents an "Outline for a Book," referring to Jesus as "the man for others." In an unpublished manuscript, *Jesus the Mime: A New Look at the Imitation of Christ,* and a published album of three cassettes, "Communication for Planned Servanthood" (Pittsburgh: Thesis Theological Cassettes, 1983), I have adapted Bonhoeffer's phrase as "the One for others" and related it to "the Son of Man" [Child of Humanity].

5. Bonhoeffer, *Letters and Papers*, 382-83.

6. Inscription on Gandhi's place of cremation at Rajghat, quoted in Kenneth Leech, *Soul Friend* (San Francisco: Harper & Row, 1977), 192.

7. See Emmanuel Levinas, *Difficult Freedom*, trans. Sean Hand (Baltimore: Johns Hopkins University Press, 1991).

8. Henry Suso, *The Exemplar*, vol. 2, trans. Sister M. Ann Edward (Dubuque: The Priory Press, 1962), 288.

9. Karl Barth, quoted in Kenneth Leech, *True Prayer* (San Francisco: Harper & Row, 1980), 68.

10. Dietrich Bonhoeffer, *Life Together* (New York: Harper & Row, 1954), 87.

11. Marjorie Thompson, "Wasting Time with God," *Weavings* 4, no. 2 (March-April 1989): 27-32.

Chapter 16

1. Henri J. M. Nouwen, *The Living Reminder* (New York: Cross-road-Seabury Press, 1977), 43-54.

2. See Louis M. Savary and Patricia H. Berne, *Kything: The Art of Spiritual Presence* (Mahwah, N.J.: Paulist Press, 1988).

3. Robert Greenleaf, *Servant Leadership* (Mahwah, N.J.: Paulist Press, 1977), 253.

4. Anthony de Mello, S.J., *Contact with God* (P.O. Box 70, Anand, 388 001, India: Gujarat Sahitya Prakash, 1990), 82-83.

5. Walter Wink, "Waging Spiritual Warfare *with the* Powers," *Weavings* 5, no. 2 (March-April 1990): 40.

6. Adapted from Flannery O'Connor, *Mystery and Manners*, ed. Sally and Robert Fitzgerald (New York: Farrar, Straus & Giroux, 1969), 133.

7. Shusaku Endo, *A Life of Jesus,* trans. Richard A. Schuchert, (Mahwah, N.J.: Paulist Press, 1973), 44; see also 57, 71, 83, 109.

8. Ibid., 42, 178.

9. Helmut Thielicke, *The Silence of God* (Grand Rapids: Eerdmans, 1962), 30-31.

Chapter 17

1. See Eddy Hall, "Do the Poor Feel Welcome in Your Church?" in *Caring for the Least of These*, ed. David Caes (Scottdale, Pa.: Herald Press, 1992), 73-80.

2. Victor Hugo, *Les Miserables,* trans. Charles E. Wilbour, abr. James K. Robinson (New York: Ballantine, Fawcett, 1961), 144-45.

3. Howard Thurman, *The Inward Journey* (Richmond, Ind. Friends United Press, 1971).

4. Robert Greenleaf, *Servant Leadership* (Mahwah, N.J.: Paulist Press, 1977), 239.

5. Robert E. Speer, in *The Hymnal for Youth* (Philadelphia: Westminster Press, 1941), 372.

Chapter 18

1. Victor Frankl, *Man's Search for Meaning* (New York: Simon & Schuster, 1969), 127.

2. Douglas Steere, *Work and Contemplation* (New York: Harper & Brothers, 1957), 57; reprinted with permission by Pendle Hill, Wallingford, Pa. 19086-6099.

3. See Howard Gardner, *Creative Minds* (New York: Basic Books, 1993).

4. I am indebted to the late Hugh T. Kerr, Jr., professor emeritus at Princeton Theological Seminary (N.J.) and editor of *Theology Today,* for the term *Calvinian.*

5. Toyohiko Kagawa, "Eien No Chibusa" [Eternal Bosom], in *Kagawa Zenshu* 20: 48; quoted in *The Princeton Seminary Bulletin* 10, no. 1, New Series (1989).

6. See Thomas Merton, "The Theology of Creativity," in *The Sacred Land,* ed. Brother Patrick Hart, *The Literary Essays of Thomas Merton* (New York: New Directions, 1985), 360.

7. John Magee, *Reality and Prayer* (New York: Harper & Brothers, 1957), 124.

8. Erik Erikson, *Gandhi's Truth* (New York: W. W. Norton, 1969), 399.

9. Alan Jones, *Exploring Spiritual Direction: An Essay on Christian Friendship* (New York: Seabury, 1983), 26-27, 85, 130.

10. *John of the Cross: Selected Writings,* ed. K. Kavanaugh, O.C.D. (Mahwah, N.J.: Paulist Press, 1987), 55-57.

11. See Robin Scroggs and Kent I. Groff, "Baptism in Mark: Dying and Rising with Christ," *Journal of Biblical Literature* 92, no. 4 (1973): 531-48.

Chapter 19

1. Urban T. Holmes, III, *Spirituality for Ministry* (Philadelphia: Westminster Press, 1983).

2. Brenda Young, "The Shaping of a Life" (unpublished paper, 1991).

3. The apostle Paul applies the idea of a hidden Messiah, which is common in rabbinic thought. Drawing on Exodus 17:6, Numbers 21:5-6, Psalm 78:15-16; 105:41, Paul identifies the very earthy experience of finding water in a rock in time of crisis as the Christ *incognito*: "And that rock was Christ" (1 Corinthians 10:4). "[Moses] considered abuse suffered *for the Christ* to be greater wealth than the treasures of Egypt," writes another author (Hebrews 11:26).

4. Abraham Maslow, *The Farther Reaches of Human Nature* (New York: Viking Press, 1971), 43.

5. Dag Hammarskjold, *Markings* (New York: Alfred A. Knopf, 1970), 197.

6. Robert Bly, *Iron John* (Redding, Mass.: Addison Wesley, 1990), 42.

Chapter 20

1. One of the finest short books on the subject is by Leslie D. Weatherhead, *The Will of God* (Nashville: Abingdon, 1972).

2. For a similar thought, see Le Ly Hayslip, *When Heaven and Earth Changed Places* (New York: Penguin, 1990).

3. See the quotation at the beginning of chapter 20 (above), from Frederick Buechner, *Wishful Thinking: A Theological ABC* (San Francisco: Harper & Row, 1973), 95.

4. Robert Frost, "Two Tramps in Mud Time," in *12 Poets*, ed. Glenn Leggett (New York: Holt, Rinehart, Winston, 1960), 264.

5. I follow the KJV: "If your eye is *single* . . . " (Greek *haplos*). The rabbis spoke of "the singling of the eye"; it means "singleness of heart," an undivided vision, focused on the one thing necessary.

6. The question is from Richard Nelson Bolles, *What Color Is Your Parachute? A Practical Manual for Job Hunters & Career-Changers* (Berkeley, Calif.: Ten Speed Press, 1993). This is an excellent resource. This two-part life-mission statement includes all elements of Bolles's *three*. See "How to Find Your Mission in Life," 355-75.

7. See Parker Palmer, "The Clearness Committee," *Weavings* 3, no. 6 (November-December 1988).

8. See Dorothy Sayers, *The Mind of the Maker* (New York: Harcourt, Brace, 1941). Sayers bases her analogy on a thought from Berdyaev in *The Destiny of Man*.

The Alban Institute:
an invitation to membership

The Alban Institute, begun in 1979, believes that the congregation is essential to the task of equipping the people of God to minister in the church and the world. A multi-denominational membership organization, the Institute provides on-site training, educational programs, consulting, research, and publishing for hundreds of churches across the country.

The Alban Institute invites you to be a member of this partnership of laity, clergy, and executives—a partnership that brings together people who are raising important questions about congregational life and people who are trying new solutions, making new discoveries, finding a new way of getting clear about the task of ministry. The Institute exists to provide you with the kinds of information and resources you need to support your ministries.

Join us now and enjoy these benefits:

CONGREGATIONS, The Alban Journal, a highly respected journal published six times a year, to keep you up to date on current issues and trends.

Inside Information, Alban's quarterly newsletter, keeps you informed about research and other happenings around Alban. Available to members only.

Publications Discounts:

- ☐ 15% for Individual, Retired Clergy, and Seminarian Members
- ☐ 25% for Congregational Members
- ☐ 40% for Judicatory and Seminary Executive Members

Discounts on Training and Education Events

Write our Membership Department at the address below or call us at (202) 244-7320 for more information about how to join The Alban Institute's growing membership, particularly about Congregational Membership in which 12 designated persons receive all benefits of membership.

The Alban Institute, Inc.
Suite 433, North
4550 Montgomery Avenue
Bethesda, MD 20814